Model Conservation Easement and Historic Preservation Easement, 1996

Revised Easements and Commentary from
The Conservation Easement Handbook

Thomas S. Barrett

Stefan Nagel

Land Trust Alliance

Copyright ©1996 Land Trust Alliance. "Model Historic Preservation Easement and Commentary" is copyright © 1996 Stefan Nagel. Permission is granted to reproduce the model easement documents or sections thereof in drafting easements.

Printed in the United States of America.

The Land Trust Alliance is the national organization of land trusts, working to ensure that they have the information, skills, and resources they need to save land through voluntary land conservation.

Land Trust Alliance
1331 H. Street, NW, Suite 400
Washington, DC 20005
202-638-4725

This publication is designed to provide accurate, authoritative information in regard to the subject matter covered. It is sold with the understanding that the publisher is not engaged in rendering legal, accounting, or other professional service. If legal advice or other expert assistance is required, the services of experienced professional advisors should be sought.

We are very grateful to the following foundations for their support of this publication: National Fish and Wildlife Foundation, MARPAT Foundation, Inc., The Mary A. Crocker Trust, Claneil Foundation, Inc., and Lennox Foundation.

Katherine Barton, Project Manager and Editor
Judith Barrett Graphics, Design and Production
Printed on recycled paper.

Model Conservation Easement and Historic Preservation Easement, 1996

Revised Easements and Commentary from
The Conservation Easement Handbook

Contents

Acknowledgements vi

Preface ix

1. Model Conservation Easement and Commentary 1

    Introduction 1

    Checklists 6

    Model Conservation Easement 12

    Commentary 24

2. Model Historic Preservation Easement and Commentary 91

    Introduction 91

    Checklists 92

    Model Historic Preservation Easement 95

    Commentary 108

Acknowledgements

The authors would like to thank attorneys David Anderson (Land Trust for Santa Barbara County, CA), Thomas A. Coughlin (Washington, DC), Andrew C. Dana (Bozeman, MT), Thomas F. Haensly (Camano Island, WA), William Ginsberg (Hofstra University School of Law, NY), Stephen J. Small (Boston, MA), and James P. Wyse (Schenk, Price, Smith, and King, NJ), who provided critical legal review and devoted many hours to this project.

Carol Wyant (National Trust for Historic Preservation, DC) rendered invaluable assistance in refining and forwarding an easement questionnaire to statewide historic preservation organizations. Story Clark (Jackson Hole Land Trust, WY) reviewed and offered in-depth comments on the conservation easement; Mary Ellen Boelhower (Society for the Protection of New Hampshire Forests), Constance Best (Pacific Forest Trust, CA), and Laurie Wayburn (Pacific Forest Trust, CA) reviewed and critiqued the conservation easement's forestry provision, and Leslie Gillette (The Nature Conservancy, Midwest Region, MN) reviewed hazardous waste language.

A special debt of gratitude is owed to Stewart Schwartz, an attorney in Alexandria, VA, who did yeoman's work organizing the voluminous and diffuse materials and documents that were reviewed for this project, sifted through a mountain of primary and secondary legal sources, and provided first-rate legal research on issues relating to the conservation easement.

Thanks are also due to Katherine Barton, former vice-president of the Land Trust Alliance, whose cheerful assistance, cajoling, and editing brought this publication to fruition.

Finally, this publication would not have been possible without the critiques, sample documents, and insights provided by individuals and organizations across the country, including:

Glenn Alex (California State Coastal Conservancy)

Leslie Ratley-Beach (Vermont Land Trust)

Robert Berner (Marin Agricultural Land Trust, CA)

Thomas Bailey (Little Traverse Conservancy, MI)

Dennis Bidwell (American Farmland Trust, DC)

Kingsbury Browne (MA)

Jeremiah Cosgrove (American Farmland Trust, NY)
Paul Edmondson (National Trust for Historic Preservation, DC)
George Covington (Gardner, Carton and Douglas, IL)
Paul Doscher (Society for the Protection of New Hampshire Forests)
Tom Hahn (Openlands Project / Corlands, IL)
Susan Hamilton (Vermont Land Trust)
Camilla Herlevich (North Carolina Coastal Land Trust)
John Hoffnagel (Napa County Land Trust, CA)
Thomas Howe (Lakes Region Conservation Trust, NH)
Julie Johnson (Anchorage Historic Properties, AK)
Joe King (Parks & Preserves Foundation, CA)
Robert Knight (Knight, Maclay, & Masar, MT)
Nelson Lee (Trust for Public Land, CA)
Joel Lerner (Executive Office of Environmental Affairs, Commonwealth of Massachusetts)
Jim Libby (Vermont Housing and Conservation Board)
Konrad Liegel (Preston, Gates, and Ellis, WA)
Gil Livingston (Vermont Land Trust)
Karin Marchetti-Kaiser (Bernard, ME)
Julie Moore (Tallahassee, FL)
Doug Muir (Garrity, Levin, & Muir, MA)
Alan Musselman (Lancaster Farmland Trust, PA)
Richard Nettler (Robins, Kaplan, Miller & Ciresi, DC)
Allen Olson (Piedmont Environmental Council, VA)
Geoff Rich (Jackson Hole Land Trust, WY)
Rock Ringling (Montana Land Reliance)
Chuck Roe (Conservation Trust for North Carolina)
Tom Saunders (Maryland Environmental Trust)
David Shields (Brandywine Conservancy, PA)
Simon Sidamon-Eristoff (Rails to Trails, DC)
Ed Thompson (American Farmland Trust, DC)
Sarah Thorne (Society for the Protection of New Hampshire Forests)
Philip Tabas (The Nature Conservancy, Eastern Region, MA)
The Trustees of Reservations, MA
Margaret Waldock (American Farmland Trust, DC)
Jeff Winegard (American Farmland Trust, DC)

The authors offer their sincerest thanks to all these individuals and organizations.

Preface

Thomas S. Barrett
Stefan Nagel

In his introduction to the original model easements in *The Conservation Easement Handbook*, noted land conservation lawyer and author Russ Brenneman spoke of the advancements in the collective knowledge of the land conservation and historic preservation community that had occurred in twenty years, and would occur in twenty more. The latter, he predicted, would "rest in no small measure on the experience of the users of this handbook." He was right, of course, but as this revision of the model easements surely illustrates, eight years has been time enough to prove it.

Since the *Handbook*'s publication in 1988, the growth of the land trust movement, by then already nothing short of phenomenal, has continued unabated. From 750 land trusts in 1988 to over 1,100 in 1996, the rate has been one new land trust every week. The number of historic preservation organizations has also increased rapidly. Love of the land and respect for history are, of course, what drive people to become involved in land saving and historic preservation. But of all the social, legal, and political tools available for translating that love and respect into concrete action—into property actually saved—none in recent years has had anywhere near the impact of the conservation easement. Easement-protected acreage under land trust stewardship increased by 250 percent from 1988 to 1994, to 737,000 acres, in the process supplanting fee acquisition as the primary land protection tool. The *Handbook* helped to make the conservation easement—considered a novel, even esoteric idea not so long ago—accessible; users of the *Handbook* have, in turn, been putting it to work at an unprecedented pace.

The Revised Model Conservation Easement

Polling a broad cross section of practitioners, the Land Trust Alliance found, gratifyingly, general satisfaction with the model conservation easement and commentary. Designed as a guide to assist people in thinking through the often quite challenging problems easement drafting can pose, the model conservation easement is working as intended. Across the country, despite variations in laws, customs, and concerns that can alter the content and appearance of the final product to a significant degree, there is nearly universal agreement that the model conservation easement represents a most useful starting point for analysis, as well as a singularly helpful and reliable reference tool.

Which is not to say there is a lack of ideas for improving it. The original model conservation easement reflected the latest thinking as of 1988. In the eight years since, people have gained a great deal of new experience drafting, negotiating, managing, and enforcing easements—experience that needs to be shared. There have been some important legal developments too—the issue of hazardous waste liability, for one—that need to be assimilated. And, as always, there are emerging questions and concerns begging to be addressed.

The revised model conservation easement and commentary take all of this into account. To give due regard to the supreme virtue of stability in matters touching on land law, the approach taken is conservative; while there is something new on virtually every page, changes to the model document itself are relatively few. Of these, new language dealing with hazardous waste liability (paragraphs 8.3-8.6) is by far the most significant.*

Other examples: paragraph 9.3 on condemnation has been changed to conform to the prevailing practice of providing in advance for the distribution of proceeds; the attorney's fees clause (paragraph 6.6) is now unilateral in favor of grantee (a reciprocal alternative is set out in the commentary); grantee's inspection rights now include a right of entry without notice where necessary to prevent, terminate, or mitigate a violation (paragraph 2(b)); and a recital of the grantee's commitment to enforce the easement for the benefit of the public at large has been deleted to avoid any suggestion of an intention to create third party standing to compel enforcement. Other changes are of the touch-up variety, a clarifying term here, a rewording there, or, as in the remedies section (paragraphs 6.1-6.9), material has been reorganized to improve readability. The bulk of the changes, though, are in the supplementary provisions and the commentary.

A key feature of this revision is the addition of numerous new examples of supplementary or alternative language. There are: a new mediation clause (supplementary paragraph 5.3); a completely revised treatment of subordination, with three sample clauses and a sample subordination agreement (supplementary paragraph 10/11; commentary section 45); additional public benefit recitals (commentary section 6); an example of cross-easement language applicable to appurtenant easements (commentary section 11); alternative purpose language for multipurpose easements (commentary section 12); language to deal with trespasser violations (commentary section 22); a cross-indemnity provision (commentary section 27); clauses dealing with economic hardship as a potential ground for extinguishment and with merger (commentary section 28); new language to deal with the emerging issue of development rights transfers and cluster zoning (commentary section 15); and more. Every section of the commentary has been revised and expanded to reflect current thinking and recent developments.

As practice in this area becomes more sophisticated, of course, expectations rise, and the strength of certain preferences and opinions becomes more intense. Approaches diverge, sometimes widely; disagreement among practitioners on some issues is entrenched. With regard to the restrictive provisions, in particular,

---

*Although proposed legislation in Congress could obviate the need for these provisions under most circumstances, with passage uncertain, caution counsels their inclusion in the model.

fact-dependent as they are, the potential variety is, for all practical purposes, limitless. It ought to come as no surprise, therefore, that there is no attempt in the model to please everybody; that way lies incoherence, at best. Nor is there any pretense that the model represents that ever illusive ideal, the single right way. Experienced hands know that drafters of conservation easements must exercise judgment at every turn. The model's purpose is to lend encouragement and support to this exercise, not supplant it.

The Model Historic Preservation Easement

Each provision of the original model historic preservation easement and its corresponding commentary has been evaluated in light of real life experience and legal developments over the last eight years. A number of organizations and practitioners responded to a survey that preceded the reconsideration of the model preservation easement. Their responses, which confirmed that many organizations had adopted the original model easement in some form, as well as the comments of reviewers of the draft revisions, have been considered and in most cases addressed in the revised model.

The substantive differences between the model conservation easement and the model preservation easement stem largely from the different characteristics of the properties that each is intended to protect. Because of the construction characteristics of many historic properties, and their typical proximity to human activity and occupancy, easements on historic properties should address issues of casualty destruction, insurance, mechanic's (construction) and other liens, possible interior access by the public and representatives of the easement holding organizations, property maintenance, indemnification for injuries, and other issues, many of which are of more limited significance in the open space conservation easement context. For example, historic properties are, because of their age and construction characteristics, often in need of repair and maintenance. When does repair or routine maintenance constitute the construction of improvements and when, in turn, does the construction of improvements trigger the inconsistent use prohibitions of Treas. Reg. § 1.170-14(e)(2)?

Increased sensitivity to and experience in these and related issues have contributed to many of the changes in the revised model preservation easement. For example, a new purpose paragraph (paragraph 1) has been added. It sets out general preservation principles as these relate to the specific property. All requests for approval, possible enforcement actions, and other administrative and legal responses under the easement will be measured against the principles set out in the purpose paragraph.

The property insurance provisions (paragraph 9) have been tightened and include insurance terminology that experience has shown balances preservation and financial interests, but that could also be modified depending on the easement grantor's circumstances and the conditions of the easement grant.

In the event of casualty damage (paragraphs 7 and 8), the easement-holding organization's discretion to determine whether and under what conditions the easement would continue in effect is more limited than in the original model easement. Both parties (and, as before, the courts) are now involved. As a practical matter, if the owner seeks extinguishment of the easement because of casualty damage and the easement-holding organization does not agree, the burden is on the property owner to satisfy a court of competent jurisdiction (paragraph 23.2) that damage casualty to the property is sufficient to justify partial or complete extinguishment.

The original model preservation easement included a provision allowing the easement-holding organization to exercise "self help" by entering the property without court order to correct a perceived violation, or to remove salvageable portions of the property following casualty damage. As noted in the commentary to paragraphs 7 and 8, these provisions have not been included in this model for three reasons: (1) experience has shown that donors inevitably reject them, (2) many states do not authorize such entry rights, and (3) such entry and "self-help" rights may subject the easement holding organization to possible liability as an operator under the Comprehensive Environmental Response, Compensation, and Liability Act (CERCLA).

Because of the characteristics of those historic properties that are typically put under preservation easement, the new model attempts throughout, and especially at paragraph 18 and supplementary paragraph 26, to clarify the interrelationship of financing, construction/mechanic's, and tax liens to the continued enforceability of the preservation easement. The priority of such liens to the enforceability of the preservation easement is rendered essentially irrelevant. The model easement states that such liens may be fully enforced; however, the enforceability of the easement cannot be impaired unless state law provides otherwise. Irrespective of such provisions, the subordination provisions of supplementary paragraph 26 cannot be neglected if a preexisting mortgage or deed of trust is secured by the easement property.

The compliance certification provisions at paragraph 13 have been changed to recognize that the owner is not always in compliance with the preservation easement. The grantee may now acknowledge noncompliance if a third party, such as a prospective purchaser or lender, requests a compliance certification.

The modifications to the tax payment (paragraph 11) and government notice (paragraph 16) provisions are similar in that both now recognize that the property owner has the right and authority to dispute and challenge government notices and tax bills. The property owner is no longer required immediately to pay disputed tax bills. The original model easement required the property owner to forward copies of all government notices, demands, bills, and letters to the easement holding organization. Under the revised easement, the owner is required merely to forward copies of government notices of violations or liens.

The original model easement required that the donor share a copy of the easement appraisal with the easement holding organization. Experience has shown that property owners are often reluctant to share easement appraisals with easement grantees. To protect the easement deduction, however, the easement grantor must share the easement valuation in some manner with the easement holding organization to satisfy the requirements of the extinguishment provisions of Treas. Reg. § 1.170A-14(g)(6)(ii). Paragraph 23.1 of the revised preservation easement therefore merely requires that parties to the transaction include the easement value with the baseline documentation. To satisfy this provision, the donor may choose to share a copy of the appraisal with the easement donee, or provide a valuation summary or similar verification (such as IRS Form 8283) acknowledged by the easement appraiser.

The easement amendment provisions at paragraph 25 have been tightened to emphasize that amendments are not to be taken lightly. The amendment of an easement may involve issues of tax, charitable organization, and trust law. Arguably, in many states the negotiation and approval of easement amendments, unless limited to clarification of ambiguity or amendment of strictly technical or procedural terms, will involve third parties such as abutting property owners and/or the office of the attorney general.

Summary

Conservation easement law is still relatively uncharted territory. While the models, more compass than map, can help with orientation, today's practitioners remain pioneers, relying on each other to report what they find out there, to share their insights and anxieties. Enforcement experience is still sparse.* What there is reinforces the conviction on which the models are based: drafting is crucial. A well-crafted easement is the best defense. Be clear about the purpose of the easement, the conservation values intended for protection by it, the public benefit to be derived from it. Assume that, however benevolent the circumstances surrounding the grant, one day a hostile landowner will materialize to put it to the test. Draft accordingly.

With thanks to all those pioneers who have shared their insights and anxieties with the authors, the model conservation and preservation easements and commentaries, having been comprehensively revised and updated, are returned to the land conservation and historic preservation community in the same spirit as the originals. May they continue to contribute to the hard-won knowledge of how best to go about the business of saving our common wealth of open spaces and our irreplaceable cultural treasures.

---

*For recent cases, see *Goldmuntz v. Town of Chilmark*, 38 Mass. App. Ct. 696, 651 N.E.2d 864 (1995); *Foundation for Preservation of Historic Georgetown v. Arnold*, 651 A.2d 794 (D.C. 1994); *Bagley v. Foundation for the Preservation of Historic Georgetown*, 647 A.2d 1110 (D.C. 1994); *Historic Harrisville, Inc. v. Temple*, No. 91-E-148 (N.H. Super. Ct. Nov. 18, 1993); *Foundation for the Preservation of Historic Georgetown v. Sagalyn*, No. 90-CA10164 (D.C. Super. Ct. Nov. 29, 1993); *Foundation for the Preservation of Historic Georgetown v. Sagalyn*, No. 90-CA10164 (D.C. Super. Ct. Dec. 12, 1991); *Smith v. Jack Nicklaus Devel. Corp.*, 225 Ill. App. 3d 384, 587 N.E.2d 1243 (1992); *Lotzenhiser v. Whidbey-Camano Land Trust*, No. 91-2-00178-7 (Sup. Ct. Wa. Aug. 15, 1991); *Bennett v. Commissioner of Food and Agriculture*, 411 Mass. 1, 576 N.E.2d 1365 (1991); *French and Pickering Creeks Conservation Trust, Inc. v. Natale*, No. 89-09574 (Chester Cty. Ct. of Common Pleas, 1989) rev'd 433 Pa. Super. 640, 638 A.2d 273 (1993); *Town of Woodside v. Gava*, 213 Cal. App. 3d 488 (1989); *Racine v. United States*, 858 F.2d 506 (9th Cir. 1988); *County of Kendall v. Aurora Natl. Bank Trust*, 170 Ill. App. 3d 212, 524 N.E.2d 262 (1988); *Thomas v. Campbell*, 107 Idaho 398, P.2d 333 (1984).

1 Model Conservation Easement and Commentary

Model Conservation Easement and Commentary

Thomas S. Barrett

Introduction

The model conservation easement is an abstraction. It is not the product of negotiation on specific facts but a studious synthesis of responses by the land conservation community, on diverse facts, to recurring drafting concerns.* The intention is that it serve as a reliable standard reference on drafting issues. Of course, no one document can hope to serve as a standard for all situations. There is no way, once and for all, to fix the variables that come with context—legal jurisdiction, character of land and resources, productive uses, conservation objectives, motivation, tax planning, financial terms, degree of governmental involvement, to name the most obvious. The model's function is not to provide a solution to the puzzle each easement transaction presents but to offer an analytical framework for solving the puzzle on its own terms. It is a guide, not a rule; one approach among many.

The Checklists: A Key to Structure

The emphasis is on structure. As the checklists that follow illustrate, the model is constructed of a succession of overlaying provisions that can be grouped according to the nature of the concerns they address. In its most fundamental form, a conservation easement is a straightforward conveyance, and Checklist II indicates the essential terms. Early easements contained little else. As experience with managing conservation easements has developed over the years, however, the terms of the instrument have evolved. While a simple conveyance might be adequate in certain rare cases today, it will fall short wherever bilateral rights and obligations—or income, estate, or gift tax considerations—come into play.

---

*In the course of preparing the original model easement and commentary, published in 1988, the author reviewed over 100 conservation easements, considered responses by some 40 practitioners to a questionnaire on the subject, and consulted directly with more than 20 recognized authorities in this field, including representatives of conservation organizations, governmental agencies, and the private bar. The 1996 revision draws on the detailed comments, recommendations, and sample easements submitted by some 45 practitioners and legal experts.

Analogous to what occurred in the development of real property leasing law, the conservation easement has, over time, taken on the characteristics of a contract as well as a conveyance. A conservation easement creates a relationship of shared control over the future of land. The perpetual nature of that relationship, designed as it is to outlast the original parties, suggests the need for a governing document in which predictable points of potential friction are anticipated and provided for and in which behavioral ground rules—for the grantee as well as the grantor—are established. These are contractual considerations, and Checklist III indicates the provisions in the model that are intended to address them.

At the same time, perpetuity counsels flexibility—the need for a mechanism for adapting to the unforeseen, a capacity for stretch. An easement is more than the sum of its restrictions; it is a right to protect certain values that inhere in a given parcel of land—its natural, scenic, open space, historical, educational, or recreational qualities. The more drafters focus on the future, which cannot be known, the more emphasis they place on articulating those values in the easement. As critical for an easement's long-term enforceability as its express restrictions, the thinking goes, is the clarity with which its protective purpose and intent are set out. The provisions that are most indicative of purpose and intent are shown in Checklist IV.

Finally, unless a fair market value purchase is involved, income, gift, or estate tax considerations are likely to be an issue, and the Internal Revenue Service's detailed requirements will, accordingly, have to be addressed. Provisions responsive to the IRS requirements are outlined in Checklist V.*

Drafting to Fit the Facts

The model is not exhaustive. There are bound to be concerns, on some facts, that it does not address. Likewise, some of the concerns it does address may not be an issue in some cases. As for the language chosen, there is no magic to it. Even the IRS, though it does require certain provisions, does not require any particular language. Drafters of legal documents develop their own individual styles, and the model in no way seeks to impose the author's. The shared goal, an elusive one, is formal clarity. Rare is the document that cannot be improved upon in this regard. The hope is that even where the model falls short of the goal, the commitment to pursuing it will be sufficiently apparent to serve as a source of encouragement to others.

Ultimately, the facts determine what should go into an easement. Some terms are more fact-dependent than others, though, and they are the hardest to deal with in a model intended for general application. Recitals of specific conservation values, and the express restrictions and reservations, are inextricable from the

---

*Not included, for obvious reasons, is a checklist of provisions addressing the multifarious state real property, income tax, and property tax laws, though such provisions, tailored to a given jurisdiction's unique requirements, represent an additional essential overlay that practitioners must take into account.

facts—a distinction that the model calls attention to by leaving them out. They are dealt with, instead, in the commentary. In an easement negotiation, the parties, for good reason, are likely to focus more on the express restrictions than any other aspect of the agreement—particularly if they are negotiating an easement where potentially competing interests require a careful balancing of permitted and prohibited uses. Accordingly, the commentary devotes considerable space to the discussion of hypothetical restrictions. It should be understood, however, that there is such a wide disparity of views on how to approach the drafting of these provisions—resulting mostly from the wide divergence of objectives people bring to them—that there is little in the way of real substantive guidance to pass on. As discussed in the commentary (comment 15), the sample restrictions strive for two virtues: balance and coherence. Beyond that—like everything else in the easement, but more so—drafters have to think it all through for themselves, carefully, critically, case by case.

Trial and Error

People who work in this field are aware that, in terms of the legal development of the concept, they are present at the creation of the conservation easement. State enabling statutes are all of relatively recent vintage and there is little case law to speak of, which makes these, to say the least, "interesting times." But newness can be a blessing as well as a curse. The opportunity to shape the concept, to give it definition, is an exciting one, and drafters should be stimulated by the fact that, in a real sense, the conservation easement is, for now at least, whatever they say it is. There will be mistakes, of course, unavoidably, and as the concept matures and the courts become more involved, there will be a welcome narrowing of approaches, and the lines of a "right way" will become clearer.

The process, though, will take time and will involve—day by day, year by year—practitioners learning, by trial and error, what it is an easement can and cannot do. All the while, their understanding of the land and the relationship of people to the land—and through the land, to each other—will be deepening, to the end that future generations may benefit not only from the open spaces they protected but from their hard-won knowledge of how—and how not—to go about it. If the model conservation easement and commentary contribute, in however small a way, to the winning of that knowledge, they will have served their purpose.

Checklists

Checklist I
Model Conservation Easement
Complete Outline*

CAPTION (Parties and Date)

RECITALS

- Title Representation/Legal Description of Property
- Generic Conservation Values
- Qualitative Description of Property
- Baseline Documentation
- Continuation of Existing Uses
- Conveyance of Right to Protect Conservation Values
- Qualifications of Grantee

GRANT

PROVISIONS

1. Purpose
2. Rights of Grantee
   (a) Protection of Conservation Values
   (b) Right of Entry for Inspection
   (c) Enforcement (Including Restoration)
3. Prohibited Uses
   [Insert Express Restrictions]
4. Reserved Rights
   [Insert Express Reservations, if desired]
5. Notice and Approval
5.1 Notice of Intention to Undertake Certain Permitted Actions
5.2 Grantee's Approval
6. Grantee's Remedies
6.1 Notice of Violation; Corrective Action
6.2 Injunctive Relief
6.3 Damages
6.4 Emergency Enforcement
6.5 Scope of Relief
6.6 Costs of Enforcement
6.7 Forbearance
6.8 Waiver of Certain Defenses
6.9 Acts Beyond Grantors' Control
7. Access
8. Costs, Liabilities, Taxes, and Environmental Compliance
8.1 Costs, Legal Requirements, and Liabilities

- 8.2 Taxes
- 8.3 Representations and Warranties
- 8.4 Remediation
- 8.5 Control
- 8.6 Hold Harmless
- 9. Extinguishment and Condemnation
- 9.1 Extinguishment
- 9.2 Valuation
- 9.3 Condemnation
- 9.4 Application of Proceeds
- 10. Assignment
- 11. Subsequent Transfers
- 12. Estoppel Certificates
- 13. Notices
- 14. Recordation
- 15. General Provisions
- 15.1 Controlling Law
- 15.2 Liberal Construction
- 15.3 Severability
- 15.4 Entire Agreement
- 15.5 No Forfeiture
- 15.6 Joint Obligation
- 15.7 Successors
- 15.8 Termination of Rights and Obligations
- 15.9 Captions
- 15.10 Counterparts

HABENDUM

SIGNATURES AND ACKNOWLEDGEMENTS

SCHEDULE OF EXHIBITS

SUPPLEMENTARY PROVISIONS**

- [5.3] Arbitration
- [5.3] Mediation
- [Between 9 and 10] Amendment
- [Between 10 and 11] Executory Limitation
- [Between 10 and 11] Subordination

---

*This is a generic outline; formal requirements for a conservation easement vary from state to state, reflecting the particular state real property, income tax, and property tax laws that a drafter must take into account.

**The designation of these provisions as "supplementary" is not meant to imply that everything else is essential, but only that a decision to include them is likely to turn more on particular facts or involve stronger preferences than the other provisions.

Checklist II
The Essentials of Conveyance*

CAPTION (Parties and Date)

RECITALS

- Title Representation/Legal Description of Property

GRANT

PROVISIONS

    1. Purpose
    2(b) Right of Entry for Inspection
    3. Prohibited Uses
    4. Reserved Rights
    7. Access (if desired)
    15.7 Successors (and Run with the Land)

HABENDUM

SIGNATURES AND ACKNOWLEDGEMENTS

SUPPLEMENTARY PROVISIONS

    [Between 10 and 11] Executory Limitation (if desired)

---

*Other provisions may be required by state law.

Checklist III
Additional Covenants
Ground Rules for a Perpetual Relationship

PROVISIONS

- 2(b) Right of Entry for Inspection (Prior Notice)
- 5. Notice and Approval
- 5.1 Notice of Intention to Undertake Certain Permitted Actions
- 5.2 Grantee's Approval
- 6. Grantee's Remedies
- 6.1 Notice of Violation; Corrective Action
- 6.2 Injunctive Relief
- 6.3 Damages
- 6.4 Emergency Enforcement
- 6.5 Scope of Relief
- 6.6 Costs of Enforcement
- 6.7 Forbearance
- 6.8 Waiver of Certain Defenses
- 6.9 Acts Beyond Grantors' Control
- 8. Costs, Liabilities, Taxes, and Environmental Compliance
- 8.1 Costs, Legal Requirements, and Liabilities
- 8.2 Taxes
- 8.3 Representations and Warranties
- 8.4 Remediation
- 8.5 Control
- 8.6 Hold Harmless
- 9. Extinguishment and Condemnation
- 9.1 Extinguishment
- 9.2 Valuation
- 9.3 Condemnation
- 10. Assignment
- 11. Subsequent Transfers
- 12. Estoppel Certificates
- 13. Notices
- 14. Recordation
- 15. General Provisions
- 15.1 Controlling Law
- 15.2 Liberal Construction
- 15.3 Severability
- 15.4 Entire Agreement
- 15.5 No Forfeiture
- 15.6 Joint Obligation
- 15.8 Termination of Rights and Obligations

15.9   Captions
15.10 Counterparts

SUPPLEMENTARY PROVISIONS

[5.3] Arbitration
[5.3] Mediation
[Between 9 and 10] Amendment
[Between 10 and 11] Subordination

Checklist IV
Clarifying Terms
Purpose and Intent

RECITALS

- Qualitative Description of Property (Conservation Values/Public Benefit)
- Baseline Documentation
- Continuation of Existing Uses
- Conveyance of Right to Protect Conservation Values

PROVISIONS

1. Purpose
2. Rights of Grantee
   (a) Protection of Conservation Values
   (c) Enforcement (Consistency)
3. Prohibited Uses
4. Reserved Rights
15.2 Liberal Construction

Checklist V
Provisions Relating to IRS Requirements*
(Treas. Reg. § 1.170A-14)

RECITALS

- Generic Conservation Values
- Qualitative Description of Property (Conservation Values/Governmental Policy/Public Benefit)
- Baseline Documentation
- Qualifications of Grantee

GRANT (Perpetuity)

PROVISIONS

1. Purpose
2(b) Right of Entry for Inspection
3. Prohibited Uses (No Inconsistent Use; No Surface Mining)
5.1 Notice of Intention to Undertake Certain Permitted Actions
6.2 Injunctive Relief (Including Restoration)
6.3 Damages
7. Access
9.1 Extinguishment
9.2 Valuation
10. Assignment
14. Recordation

SUPPLEMENTARY PROVISIONS

[Between 10 and 11] Subordination

---

*The requirements of Treas. Reg. § 1.170A-14 must be met for an easement gift to be deductible for income tax purposes. Treas. Reg. § 25.2703-1(a)(4), governing valuation for federal estate and gift tax purposes pursuant to Section 2703 of the Internal Revenue Code, is of narrower scope in that the conservation purpose test of I.R.C. § 170(h) and Treas. Reg. 1.170A-14 need not be met. See I.R.C. §§ 2056(f), 2522(d). Other requirements, including mortgage subordination and the prohibition against surface mining, however, are the same.

Model Conservation Easement

Note: The boxed numbers inserted in the text of the easement correspond with the subheading numbers in the commentary that follows.

DEED OF CONSERVATION EASEMENT [1]

THIS GRANT DEED OF CONSERVATION EASEMENT is made this _____ day of [month], [year], by _____ and _____, husband and wife, having an address at _____ ("Grantors"), in favor of _____, a nonprofit [state of incorporation] corporation [qualified to do business in (state where property is located)], having an address at _____ _____ ("Grantee"). [2]

WITNESSETH:

WHEREAS, [3] Grantors are the sole owners in fee simple of certain real property in _____ County, [state], more particularly described in Exhibit A attached hereto and incorporated by this reference (the "Property"); and [4]

WHEREAS, the property possesses [e.g., natural, scenic, open space, historical, educational, and/or recreational] values (collectively, "conservation values") of great importance to Grantors, the people of [county, locale, or region] and the people of the State of _____; and [5]

WHEREAS, in particular, _____[describe specific conservation values]_____; and [6]

WHEREAS, the specific conservation values of the Property are further documented in an inventory of relevant features of the Property, dated _____, _[on file at the offices of Grantee—or—attached hereto as Exhibit B]_ and incorporated by this reference ("Baseline Documentation"), which consists of reports, maps, photographs, and other documentation that the parties agree provide, collectively, an accurate representation of the Property at the time of this grant and which is intended to serve as an objective, though nonexclusive, information baseline for monitoring compliance with the terms of this grant; and [7]

WHEREAS, Grantors intend that the conservation values of the Property be preserved and maintained by permitting only those land uses on the Property that do not significantly impair or interfere with them, including, without limitation, those land uses relating to _[e.g., farming, ranching, or timber production]_ existing at the time of this grant; and [8]

WHEREAS, Grantors further intend, as owners of the Property, to convey to Grantee the right to preserve and protect the conservation values of the Property in perpetuity; and [9]

WHEREAS, Grantee is a publicly supported, tax-exempt nonprofit organization and a qualified organization under Sections 501(c)(3) and 170(h), respectively, of the Internal Revenue Code of 1986, as amended, and the regulations promulgated thereunder (the "Internal Revenue Code"), whose primary purpose is [e.g., the preservation, protection, or enhancement of land in its natural, scenic, historical, agricultural, forested, and/or open space condition] ; [10]

NOW, THEREFORE, in consideration of the above and the mutual covenants, terms, conditions, and restrictions contained herein, and pursuant to the law of [state where Property is located] and in particular [specific state statutory authority] , Grantors hereby voluntarily grant and convey to Grantee a conservation easement in perpetuity over the Property of the nature and character and to the extent hereinafter set forth ("Easement"). [11]

1. **Purpose.** It is the purpose of this Easement to assure that the Property will be retained forever [predominantly] in its [e.g., natural, scenic, historical, agricultural, forested, and/or open space] condition and to prevent any use of the Property that will [significantly] impair or interfere with the conservation values of the Property. Grantors intend that this Easement will confine the use of the Property to such activities, including, without limitation, those involving [e.g., farming, ranching, timber production, public recreation, or education], as are not inconsistent with the purpose of this Easement. [12]

2. **Rights of Grantee.** To accomplish the purpose of this Easement the following rights are conveyed to Grantee by this Easement:

(a) To preserve and protect the conservation values of the Property;

(b) To enter upon the Property at reasonable times in order to monitor compliance with and otherwise enforce the terms of this Easement in accordance with section 6; provided that, except in cases where Grantee determines that immediate entry is required to prevent, terminate, or mitigate a violation of this Easement, such entry shall be upon prior reasonable notice to Grantors, and Grantee shall not in any case unreasonably interfere with Grantors' use and quiet enjoyment of the Property; and

(c) To prevent any activity on or use of the Property that is inconsistent with the purpose of this Easement and to require the restoration of such areas or features of the Property that may be damaged by any inconsistent activity or use, pursuant to the remedies set forth in section 6. [13]

3. **Prohibited Uses.** Any activity on or use of the Property inconsistent with the purpose of this Easement is prohibited. Without limiting the generality of the foregoing, the following activities and uses are expressly prohibited: [14]

[Insert Express Restrictions] [15]

4. **Reserved Rights.** Grantors reserve to themselves, and to their personal representatives, heirs, successors, and assigns, all rights accruing from their ownership of the Property, including the right to engage in, or permit or invite others

to engage in, all uses of the Property that are not expressly prohibited herein and are not inconsistent with the purpose of this Easement. [Without limiting the generality of the foregoing, and subject to the terms of paragraph 3, the following rights are expressly reserved:] [16]

[Insert Express Reservations, if desired] [17]

5. **Notice and Approval.**

5.1 **Notice of Intention to Undertake Certain Permitted Actions.** The purpose of requiring Grantors to notify Grantee prior to undertaking certain permitted activities, as provided in paragraphs _____, is to afford Grantee an adequate opportunity to monitor the activities in question to ensure that they are designed and carried out in a manner that is not inconsistent with the purpose of this Easement. Whenever notice is required Grantors shall notify Grantee in writing not less than [e.g., thirty (30)/sixty (60)] days prior to the date Grantors intend to undertake the activity in question. The notice shall describe the nature, scope, design, location, timetable, and any other material aspect of the proposed activity in sufficient detail to permit Grantee to make an informed judgment as to its consistency with the purpose of this Easement.

5.2 **Grantee's Approval.** Where Grantee's approval is required, as set forth in paragraphs _____, Grantee shall grant or withhold its approval in writing within [e.g., thirty (30)/sixty (60)] days of receipt of Grantors' written request therefor. Grantee's approval may be withheld only upon a reasonable determination by Grantee that the action as proposed would be inconsistent with the purpose of this Easement. [18]

6. **Grantee's Remedies.**

6.1 **Notice of Violation; Corrective Action.** If Grantee determines that a violation of the terms of this Easement has occurred or is threatened, Grantee shall give written notice to Grantors of such violation and demand corrective action sufficient to cure the violation and, where the violation involves injury to the Property resulting from any use or activity inconsistent with the purpose of this Easement, to restore the portion of the Property so injured to its prior condition in accordance with a plan approved by Grantee.

6.2 **Injunctive Relief.** If Grantors fail to cure the violation within [e.g., thirty (30)] days after receipt of notice thereof from Grantee, or under circumstances where the violation cannot reasonably be cured within a [thirty (30)] day period, fail to begin curing such violation within the [thirty (30)] day period, or fail to continue diligently to cure such violation until finally cured, Grantee may bring an action at law or in equity in a court of competent jurisdiction to enforce the terms of this Easement, to enjoin the violation, *ex parte* as necessary, by temporary or permanent injunction, and to require the restoration of the Property to the condition that existed prior to any such injury.

6.3 **Damages.** Grantee shall be entitled to recover damages for violation of the terms of this Easement or injury to any conservation values protected by this Easement, including, without limitation, damages for the loss of scenic, aesthetic, or environmental values. Without limiting Grantors' liability therefor, Grantee, in its sole discretion, may apply any damages recovered to the cost of undertaking any corrective action on the Property.

6.4 **Emergency Enforcement.** If Grantee, in its sole discretion, determines that circumstances require immediate action to prevent or mitigate significant damage to the conservation values of the Property, Grantee may pursue its remedies under this section 6 without prior notice to Grantors or without waiting for the period provided for cure to expire.

6.5 **Scope of Relief.** Grantee's rights under this section 6 apply equally in the event of either actual or threatened violations of the terms of this Easement. Grantors agree that Grantee's remedies at law for any violation of the terms of this Easement are inadequate and that Grantee shall be entitled to the injunctive relief described in paragraph 6.2, both prohibitive and mandatory, in addition to such other relief to which Grantee may be entitled, including specific performance of the terms of this Easement, without the necessity of proving either actual damages or the inadequacy of otherwise available legal remedies. Grantee's remedies described in this section 6 shall be cumulative and shall be in addition to all remedies now or hereafter existing at law or in equity. [19]

6.6 **Costs of Enforcement.** All reasonable costs incurred by Grantee in enforcing the terms of this Easement against Grantors, including, without limitation, costs and expenses of suit and reasonable attorneys' fees, and any costs of restoration necessitated by Grantors' violation of the terms of this Easement shall be borne by Grantors; provided, however, that if Grantors ultimately prevail in a judicial enforcement action each party shall bear its own costs. [20]

6.7 **Forbearance.** Forbearance by Grantee to exercise its rights under this Easement in the event of any breach of any term of this Easement by Grantors shall not be deemed or construed to be a waiver by Grantee of such term or of any subsequent breach of the same or any other term of this Easement or of any of Grantee's rights under this Easement. No delay or omission by Grantee in the exercise of any right or remedy upon any breach by Grantors shall impair such right or remedy or be construed as a waiver.

6.8 **Waiver of Certain Defenses.** Grantors hereby waive any defense of laches, estoppel, or prescription. [21]

6.9 **Acts Beyond Grantors' Control.** Nothing contained in this Easement shall be construed to entitle Grantee to bring any action against Grantors for any injury to or change in the Property resulting from causes beyond Grantors' control, including, without limitation, fire, flood, storm, and earth movement, or from any prudent action taken by Grantors under emergency conditions to prevent, abate, or mitigate significant injury to the Property resulting from such causes. [22]

7. **Access.** No right of access by the general public to any portion of the Property is conveyed by this Easement. [23]

8. Costs, Liabilities, Taxes, and Environmental Compliance.

8.1 Costs, Legal Requirements, and Liabilities. Grantors retain all responsibilities and shall bear all costs and liabilities of any kind related to the ownership, operation, upkeep, and maintenance of the Property, including the maintenance of adequate liability insurance coverage. Grantors remain solely responsible for obtaining any applicable governmental permits and approvals for any construction or other activity or use permitted by this Easement, and all such construction or other activity or use shall be undertaken in accordance with all applicable federal, state, and local laws, regulations, and requirements. Grantors shall keep the Property free of any liens arising out of any work performed for, materials furnished to, or obligations incurred by Grantors. [24]

8.2 Taxes. Grantors shall pay before delinquency all taxes, assessments, fees, and charges of whatever description levied on or assessed against the Property by competent authority (collectively "taxes"), including any taxes imposed upon, or incurred as a result of, this Easement, and shall furnish Grantee with satisfactory evidence of payment upon request. [25]

8.3 Representations and Warranties. Grantors represent and warrant that, after reasonable investigation and to the best of their knowledge:

(a) No substance defined, listed, or otherwise classified pursuant to any federal, state, or local law, regulation, or requirement as hazardous, toxic, polluting, or otherwise contaminating to the air, water, or soil, or in any way harmful or threatening to human health or the environment exists or has been released, generated, treated, stored, used, disposed of, deposited, abandoned, or transported in, on, from, or across the Property;

(b) There are not now any underground storage tanks located on the Property, whether presently in service or closed, abandoned, or decommissioned, and no underground storage tanks have been removed from the Property in a manner not in compliance with applicable federal, state, and local laws, regulations, and requirements;

(c) Grantors and the Property are in compliance with all federal, state, and local laws, regulations, and requirements applicable to the Property and its use;

(d) There is no pending or threatened litigation in any way affecting, involving, or relating to the Property; and

(e) No civil or criminal proceedings or investigations have been instigated at any time or are now pending, and no notices, claims, demands, or orders have been received, arising out of any violation or alleged violation of, or failure to comply with, any federal, state, or local law, regulation, or requirement applicable to the Property or its use, nor do there exist any facts or circumstances that Grantors might reasonably expect to form the basis for any such proceedings, investigations, notices, claims, demands, or orders.

8.4 Remediation. If, at any time, there occurs, or has occurred, a release in, on, or about the Property of any substance now or hereafter defined, listed, or otherwise classified pursuant to any federal, state, or local law, regulation, or requirement as hazardous, toxic, polluting, or otherwise contaminating to the air, water, or soil, or in any way harmful or threatening to human health or the environment, Grantors agree to take all steps necessary to assure its containment and remediation, including any cleanup that may be required, unless the release was caused by Grantee, in which case Grantee shall be responsible therefor.

8.5 **Control.** Nothing in this Easement shall be construed as giving rise, in the absence of a judicial decree, to any right or ability in Grantee to exercise physical or managerial control over the day-to-day operations of the Property, or any of Grantors' activities on the Property, or otherwise to become an operator with respect to the Property within the meaning of The Comprehensive Environmental Response, Compensation, and Liability Act of 1980, as amended ("CERCLA"), and [corresponding state statute] . [26]

8.6 **Hold Harmless.** Grantors hereby release and agree to hold harmless, indemnify, and defend Grantee and its members, directors, officers, employees, agents, and contractors and the heirs, personal representatives, successors, and assigns of each of them (collectively "Indemnified Parties") from and against any and all liabilities, penalties, fines, charges, costs, losses, damages, expenses, causes of action, claims, demands, orders, judgments, or administrative actions, including, without limitation, reasonable attorneys' fees, arising from or in any way connected with: (1) injury to or the death of any person, or physical damage to any property, resulting from any act, omission, condition, or other matter related to or occurring on or about the Property, regardless of cause, unless due solely to the negligence of any of the Indemnified Parties; (2) the violation or alleged violation of, or other failure to comply with, any state, federal, or local law, regulation, or requirement, including, without limitation, CERCLA and [corresponding state statute], by any person other than any of the Indemnified Parties, in any way affecting, involving, or relating to the Property; (3) the presence or release in, on, from, or about the Property, at any time, of any substance now or hereafter defined, listed, or otherwise classified pursuant to any federal, state, or local law, regulation, or requirement as hazardous, toxic, polluting, or otherwise contaminating to the air, water, or soil, or in any way harmful or threatening to human health or the environment, unless caused solely by any of the Indemnified Parties; and (4) the obligations, covenants, representations, and warranties of paragraphs 8.1 through 8.5. [27]

9. Extinguishment and Condemnation.

9.1 **Extinguishment.** If circumstances arise in the future that render the purpose of this Easement impossible to accomplish, this Easement can only be terminated or extinguished, whether in whole or in part, by judicial proceedings in a court of competent jurisdiction. The amount of the proceeds to which Grantee shall be entitled, after the satisfaction of prior claims, from any sale, exchange, or involuntary conversion of all or any portion of the Property subsequent to such termination or extinguishment, shall be the stipulated fair market value of the Easement, or proportionate part thereof, as determined in accordance with paragraph 9.2. [28]

9.2 **Valuation.** This Easement constitutes a real property interest immediately vested in Grantee, which, for the purposes of paragraph 9.1, the parties stipulate to have a fair market value determined by multiplying (1) the fair market value of the Property unencumbered by the Easement (minus any increase in value after the date of this grant attributable to improvements) by (2) [x/y , which is] the ratio of the value of the Easement at the time of this grant to the value of the Property, without deduction for the value of the Easement, at the time of this grant. [The values at the time of this grant {are—or—shall be} those values used to calculate the deduction for federal income tax purposes allowable by reason of this grant, pursuant to Section 170(h) of the Internal Revenue Code. For the purposes of this paragraph, the ratio of the value of the Easement to the value of the Property unencumbered by the Easement shall remain constant.] [29]

9.3 **Condemnation.** If all or any part of the Property is taken by exercise of the power of eminent domain or acquired by purchase in lieu of condemnation, whether by public, corporate, or other authority, so as to terminate this Easement, in whole or in part, Grantors and Grantee shall act jointly to recover the full value of the interests in the Property subject to the taking or in lieu purchase and all direct or incidental damages resulting therefrom. All expenses reasonably incurred by Grantors and Grantee in connection with the taking or in lieu purchase shall be paid out of the amount recovered. Grantee's share of the balance of the amount recovered shall be determined by multiplying that balance by the ratio set forth in paragraph 9.2. [30]

9.4 **Application of Proceeds.** Grantee shall use any proceeds received under the circumstances described in this section 9 in a manner consistent with its conservation purposes, which are exemplified by this grant. [31]

10. **Assignment.** This Easement is transferable, but Grantee may assign its rights and obligations under this Easement only to an organization that is a qualified organization at the time of transfer under Section 170(h) of the Internal Revenue Code (or any successor provision then applicable), and authorized to acquire and hold conservation easements under [state statute] (or any successor provision then applicable) or the laws of the United States. As a condition of such transfer, Grantee shall require that the conservation purpose that this grant is intended to advance continue to be carried out. Grantee agrees to give written notice to Grantors of an assignment at least [e.g., twenty (20)] days prior to the date of such assignment. The failure of Grantee to give such notice shall not affect the validity of such assignment nor shall it impair the validity of this Easement or limit its enforceability in any way. [32]

11. **Subsequent Transfers.** Grantors agree to incorporate the terms of this Easement by reference in any deed or other legal instrument by which they divest themselves of any interest in all or a portion of the Property, including, without limitation, a leasehold interest. Grantors further agree to give written notice to Grantee of the transfer of any interest at least [e.g. twenty (20)] days prior to the date of such transfer. The failure of Grantors to perform any act required by this paragraph shall not impair the validity of this Easement or limit its enforceability in any way. [33]

12. **Estoppel Certificates.** Upon request by Grantors, Grantee shall within [e.g., twenty (20)] days execute and deliver to Grantors, or to any party designated by Grantors, any document, including an estoppel certificate, which certifies, to the best of Grantee's knowledge, Grantors' compliance with any obligation of Grantors contained in this Easement or otherwise evidences the status of this Easement. Such certification shall be limited to the condition of the Property as of Grantee's most recent inspection. If Grantors request more current documentation, Grantee shall conduct an inspection, at Grantors' expense, within [e.g., thirty (30)] days of receipt of Grantors' written request therefor. [34]

13. **Notices.** Any notice, demand, request, consent, approval, or communication that either party desires or is required to give to the other shall be in writing and either served personally or sent by first class mail, postage prepaid, addressed as follows:

To Grantors: _____
_____
_____

To Grantee: _____
_____
_____

or to such other address as either party from time to time shall designate by written notice to the other. [35]

14. **Recordation.** Grantee shall record this instrument in timely fashion in the official records of _____ County, [state], and may re-record it at any time as may be required to preserve its rights in this Easement. [36]

15. **General Provisions.**

15.1 **Controlling Law.** The interpretation and performance of this Easement shall be governed by the laws of the State of [state].

15.2 **Liberal Construction.** Any general rule of construction to the contrary notwithstanding, this Easement shall be liberally construed in favor of the grant to effect the purpose of this Easement and the policy and purpose of [state statute]. If any provision in this instrument is found to be ambiguous, an interpretation consistent with the purpose of this Easement that would render the provision valid shall be favored over any interpretation that would render it invalid.

15.3 **Severability.** If any provision of this Easement, or the application thereof to any person or circumstance, is found to be invalid, the remainder of the provisions of this Easement, or the application of such provision to persons or circumstances other than those as to which it is found to be invalid, as the case may be, shall not be affected thereby.

15.4 **Entire Agreement.** This instrument sets forth the entire agreement of the parties with respect to the Easement and supersedes all prior discussions, negotiations, understandings, or agreements relating to the Easement, all of which are merged herein. [No alteration or variation of this instrument shall be valid or binding unless contained in an amendment that complies with paragraph ____. *(See supplementary provisions on amendment.)*]

15.5 **No Forfeiture.** Nothing contained herein will result in a forfeiture or reversion of Grantor's title in any respect.

15.6 **Joint Obligation.** The obligations imposed by this Easement upon Grantors shall be joint and several.

15.7 **Successors.** The covenants, terms, conditions, and restrictions of this Easement shall be binding upon, and inure to the benefit of, the parties hereto and their respective personal representatives, heirs, successors, and assigns and shall continue as a servitude running in perpetuity with the Property. The terms "Grantors" and "Grantee," wherever used herein, and any pronouns used in place thereof, shall include, respectively, the above-named Grantors and their personal representatives, heirs, successors, and assigns, and the above-named Grantee and its successors and assigns.

15.8 **Termination of Rights and Obligations.** A party's rights and obligations under this Easement terminate upon transfer of the party's interest in the Easement or Property, except that liability for acts or omissions occurring prior to transfer shall survive transfer.

15.9 **Captions.** The captions in this instrument have been inserted solely for convenience of reference and are not a part of this instrument and shall have no effect upon construction or interpretation.

15.10 **Counterparts.** The parties may execute this instrument in two or more counterparts, which shall, in the aggregate, be signed by both parties; each counterpart shall be deemed an original instrument as against any party who has signed it. In the event of any disparity between the counterparts produced, the recorded counterpart shall be controlling. [37]

TO HAVE AND TO HOLD unto Grantee, its successors, and assigns forever. [38]

IN WITNESS WHEREOF Grantors and Grantee have set their hands on the day and year first above written.

```
                    Grantors  _____
                              _____

                    Grantee   _____
                         by   _____
                         its  _____ [official capacity] ____
```

[Acknowledgments]

SCHEDULE OF EXHIBITS

A. Legal Description of Property Subject to Easement

[B. Baseline Documentation]

C. Site Descriptions/Map

[D. Mortgage Subordination Agreement] [39]

Supplementary Provisions [40]

Note: Paragraph numbers indicate relative position in model.

[5.3] **Arbitration.** If a dispute arises between the parties concerning the consistency of any proposed use or activity with the purpose of this Easement, and Grantors agree not to proceed with the use or activity pending resolution of the dispute, either party may refer the dispute to arbitration by request made in writing to the other. Within _[e.g., thirty (30)]_ days of the receipt of such a request, the parties shall select a single arbitrator to hear the matter. If the parties are unable to agree on the selection of a single arbitrator, then each party shall name one arbitrator and the two arbitrators thus selected shall select a third arbitrator; provided, however, if either party fails to select an arbitrator, or if the two arbitrators selected by the parties fail to select the third arbitrator within _[e.g., fourteen (14)]_ days after the appointment of the second arbitrator, then in each such instance a proper court, on petition of a party, shall appoint the second or third arbitrator or both, as the case may be, in accordance with _[state arbitration statute/other appropriate body of rules]_ then in effect. The matter shall be settled in accordance with _[state arbitration statute/other appropriate body of rules]_ then in effect, and a judgment on the arbitration award may be entered in any court having jurisdiction thereof. The prevailing party shall be entitled, in addition to such other relief as may be granted, to a reasonable sum as and for all its costs and expenses related to such arbitration, including, without limitation, the fees and expenses of the arbitrators and attorneys' fees, which shall be determined by the arbitrators and any court of competent jurisdiction that may be called upon to enforce or review the award. [41]

[5.3] **Mediation.** If a dispute arises between the parties concerning the consistency of any proposed use or activity with the purpose of this Easement, and Grantors agree not to proceed with the use or activity pending resolution of the dispute, either party may refer the dispute to mediation by request made in writing to the other. Within _[e.g., ten (10)]_ days of the receipt of such a request, the parties shall select a single trained and impartial mediator. If the parties are unable to agree on the selection of a single mediator, then the parties shall, within __[e.g., fifteen (15)]__ days of receipt of the initial request, jointly apply to a proper court for the appointment of a trained and impartial mediator. Mediation shall then proceed in accordance with the following guidelines:

(a) **Purpose.** The purpose of the mediation is to: (i) promote discussion between the parties; (ii) assist the parties to develop and exchange pertinent information concerning the issues in dispute; and (iii) assist the parties to develop proposals which will enable them to arrive at a mutually acceptable resolution of the controversy. The mediation is not intended to result in any express or *de facto* modification or amendment of the terms, conditions, or restrictions of this Easement.

(b) **Participation.** The mediator may meet with the parties and their counsel jointly or *ex parte*. The parties agree that they will participate in the mediation process in good faith and expeditiously, attending all sessions scheduled by the mediator. Representatives of the parties with settlement authority will attend mediation sessions as requested by the mediator.

(c) **Confidentiality.** All information presented to the mediator shall be deemed confidential and shall be disclosed by the mediator only with the consent of the parties or their respective counsel. The mediator shall not be subject to subpoena by any party. No statements made or documents prepared for mediation sessions shall be disclosed in any subsequent proceeding or construed as an admission of a party.

(d) **Time Period.** Neither party shall be obligated to continue the mediation process beyond a period of __[e.g., ninety (90)]__ days from the date of receipt of the initial request or if the mediator concludes that there is no reasonable likelihood that continuing mediation will result in a mutually agreeable resolution of the dispute.

(e) **Costs.** The costs of the mediator shall be borne equally by Grantors and Grantee; the parties shall bear their own expenses, including attorneys' fees, individually. [42]

[Between 9 and 10] **Amendment.** If circumstances arise under which an amendment to or modification of this Easement would be appropriate, Grantors and Grantee are free to jointly amend this Easement; provided that no amendment shall be allowed that will affect the qualification of this Easement or the status of Grantee under any applicable laws, including __[state statute]__ or Section 170(h) of the Internal Revenue Code, and any amendment shall be consistent with the purpose of this Easement and shall not affect its perpetual duration. Any such amendment shall be recorded in the official records of _____ County, __[state]__ . [43]

[Between 10 and 11] **Executory Limitation.** If Grantee shall cease to exist or to be a qualified organization under Section 170(h) of the Internal Revenue Code, or to be authorized to acquire and hold conservation easements under __[state statute]__, then Grantee's rights and obligations under this Easement shall become immediately vested in __[designated back-up grantee]__. If __[designated back-up grantee]__ is no longer in existence at the time the rights and obligations under this Easement would otherwise vest in it, or if [designated back-up grantee] is not qualified or authorized to hold conservation easements as provided for an assignment pursuant to paragraph 10, or if it shall refuse such rights and obligations, then the rights and obligations under this Easement shall vest in such organization as a court of competent jurisdiction shall direct pursuant to applicable [state] law and consistent with the requirements for an assignment pursuant to paragraph 10. [44]

[Between 10 and 11] **Subordination.** At the time of conveyance of this Easement, the Property is subject to a mortgage, the holder of which has agreed by separate instrument, a copy of which is attached hereto as Exhibit D and incorporated by this reference, to subordinate its rights in the Property to the extent necessary to permit the Grantee to enforce the purpose of this Easement in perpetuity and to prevent any modification or extinguishment of this Easement by the exercise of any rights of the mortgage holder. *(See sample subordination agreement in Commentary.)* [45]

Commentary

Note: The numbers at the beginning of the subheads in this section correspond with the boxed numbers inserted in the text of the model conservation easement preceding this commentary. Reference to the appropriate numbered paragraphs in the model appears in parentheses.

1. Title of Document

A deed is a written instrument for effecting the transfer of title to real property, which consists of land and interests in land. "Conservation easement" is the name used in most jurisdictions to describe the real property interest that is the subject of the instrument at hand, although in some states it may be designated, variously, a conservation, open space, or scenic easement, restriction, covenant, or servitude. The requirements for and some of the technical legal attributes of conservation interests vary from state to state.[1] It should be noted that, in some jurisdictions, use of the term "deed," though appropriate as a matter of property law, may trigger additional recording fees and raise transfer and property tax questions that would not otherwise arise. It is, of course, of fundamental importance that each conservation interest be drawn to reflect the law of the jurisdiction where the subject property is located.

2. Preliminary Identification of Parties

The date of conveyance and the current names and addresses of the original parties are given at the outset for ease of reference. The status of the parties is indicated for the same reason, to be expanded on in the recitals to follow. The phrase "husband and wife" that appears in the model is significant in the community property states of the West where both must be joined in the conveyance to effect a fully valid transfer of title to an interest in community real property. Other joint ownership relationships, such as those involving partners, joint tenants, cotenants, or tenants by the entirety (another form of title sometimes employed by marriage partners), should be indicated, as appropriate, and all necessary parties joined in the conveyance. A current title report, which should be obtained early in the process, will identify all persons and entities having an ownership interest in the property. Where the landowner is a single individual or entity, of course, the singular term "Grantor" is used. Other designations for the parties, such as "Landowner" and "Holder," may be substituted for "Grantor" and "Grantee," if preferred.

---

1. For a concise review of the law relating to conservation easements, see Richard R. Powell, *The Law of Real Property*, 34A.01-34A.07 (Matthew Bender and Co. 1993).

The nonprofit corporate status of the grantee and its state of incorporation should be shown. If the grantor is a corporation, partnership, or trust, corresponding status information should be supplied. If the state of incorporation of a grantor or grantee is different from the state in which the property is situated, depending on the jurisdiction, formal qualification to do business in the state where the property is situated may be required to effect a valid transfer. In addition, for out-of-state grantees, qualification may be an independent requirement of a state's conservation easement enabling legislation. Qualification typically involves little more than filing the corporate charter and appointing an agent for service of process. Annual informational filings preserve a corporation's good standing. The fact of qualification should be stated as indicated in brackets.

Proof of these matters, as well as of any other material precondition, should be exchanged prior to executing the easement. Proof of the IRS's determination of a grantee's public nonprofit tax exempt status is likely to be required, for example, as will proof of authority to execute the easement instrument, which will vary, in the grantor's case, according to whether a corporation, partnership, trust, or individual is involved. In the case of a corporation, for example, a resolution of the board of directors might be required. Where a governmental entity is a party, the easement should make reference to its charter or other qualifying source of authority. Closing documentation might then include a copy of any prerequisite resolution or other legislative or administrative action specifically authorizing the easement transfer. Warranties might also be given if requested.

3. Recitals (The "Whereas" Clauses)

The recitals or "whereas" clauses function as a preamble to the easement, setting forth background information essential for understanding both the legal and factual basis for its creation. Use of the conjunction "whereas" to introduce the recitals is a traditional but by no means obligatory conveyancing convention. The model follows traditional form here and elsewhere because most practitioners do. Additionally, as a practical matter, when reviewing multipage documents, being able to tell at a glance where you are at any given point is something you quickly come to appreciate, and the familiar structural guideposts, like the "whereas" introducing each recital, can be a real help. Another approach, preferred by some drafters, is to letter the recitals and number the operative provisions. Matters of style are largely governed by taste, of course. While there may be something to be gained from giving the relatively "novel" conservation easement a familiar, traditional look, a plainer style should serve just as well, assuming all substantive requirements are met.

In some jurisdictions recitals are given little if any legal effect, in which case they should be moved to the "Purpose" clause of the easement or incorporated there by reference, as illustrated in **comment 12 (Purpose)**.

4. Title Representation and Legal Description of the Property

In this first recital the grantors' "fee simple" ownership of the property indicates that they own the rights that are being transferred by means of the easement—a fact that the grantee should corroborate by a search of the property records of the county in which the property is situated. In addition to identifying ownership, a title search will reveal the existence of any recorded liens or other encumbrances on the property that might jeopardize the easement. Often landowners are willing to provide, at their own expense, a title report prepared by an attorney or title company. If not, a grantee should obtain one on its own.

The legal description of the property must be set forth and must conform exactly to the description appearing in the title records. Reference to any existing surveys and the appropriate record book and page, as well as the tax parcel number, often described by block and lot, should also be made. If the easement covers only part of a larger parcel, a survey delimiting its precise boundaries should be obtained, unless the area can be identified with sufficient legal certainty under state law by reference to existing governmental survey subdivisions or maps, photographs, or prominent natural features. Of course, as a practical matter, the easier it is to identify the land under easement on the ground, the easier it will be to administer the easement, and the boundaries of an easement should be chosen with that fact in mind. Attaching an exhibit containing the description and incorporating it by reference is a useful drafting device, particularly if the description is long or is not available during preparation of the early drafts.

In states that remain without conservation easement enabling legislation, unless the grantee already owns adjacent land, a small parcel is often carved out of the property and conveyed in fee to the grantee in order to circumvent common law limitations on the enforceability of negative easements in gross (i.e., not running to the benefit of another property). The easement is then described as "appurtenant" to the parcel conveyed in fee. This parcel, which is called the "dominant" parcel in common law parlance, must be described with the same particularity as the parcel to be burdened by the easement. Commonly, the conveyed parcel will be transferred subject to deed restrictions or a cross-easement to assure its use will be consistent with the restrictions imposed on the larger parcel. This device is discussed further in **comment 11 (Grant)**.

5. Generic Conservation Values

The generic conservation values introduced here, in brackets, mimic the conservation purpose categories of Section 170(h) of the Internal Revenue Code, which governs the deductibility of gifts of conservation easements. The conservation values of a given property might include one or more of these, or subcategories of these (e.g., agricultural or silvicultural), or other values, depending on the circumstances. Of course, only those values appropriate to the land in question should be stated, and care should be taken to assure that they meet the qualifying criteria of the Internal Revenue Code and regulations if a deduction is being sought. Similarly, any state and local requirements should be tracked.

The collective term "conservation values," introduced parenthetically here, is a pivotal term in the easement. This recital, and the detailed recitals to follow, give it defining content.

6. Qualitative Description of Property

The purpose of this paragraph, which is likely in practice to extend to several paragraphs, is to lay the foundation for the easement by summarizing, concisely, the characteristics of the subject property that have been identified for protection and the rationale for protecting them. They should be drafted with great care since they will function over time as the primary reference point for determining what the easement is all about. Each resource (and its location, if confined to a fixed area within the property) should be clearly described (a particular view to or from a mountain range, a stand of virgin timber, a critical wetland, an ocean access way, prime farmland, an historical or archaeological site) so that the parties, their successors, and if necessary, the courts—however they may differ under a given set of circumstances on how it should be achieved—will always be able to determine with some certainty the underlying purpose of the easement.

Clarity here can go a long way to compensate for a built-in limitation all easement drafters face: the impossibility of anticipating in the restrictive section of the easement every conceivable potentially conflicting variation in use of the property that might create problems in the future. This is not to say that all protected resources must be narrowly defined. Typically an easement serves broad purposes (a community's need for open space) as well as narrow (protection of significant habitat for an endangered species, for example). The point is only that an easement that is silent or vague about the resources to be protected, whether specific or general in character, may provide an inadequate level of protection for one or the other under the stress of unforeseen circumstances or a challenge to its validity.

The conservation values of the subject property should be highlighted in the context of any applicable governmental policies or programs designed to promote their protection, and the public benefit to be derived from their protection should be emphasized. Known threats to their protection, such as high development potential, might also be described. For a helpful listing of some factors that warrant mention, if applicable, see the conservation purposes section of the Internal Revenue Service conservation easement regulations found at Treasury Regulations Section 1.170A-14(d). In addition, where the parties have met requirements for qualifying the easement under a federal, state, or local program that has specific legal consequences of its own (such as, for example, automatic preferential property tax treatment), express reference to compliance with these requirements should be made here.

The content of these public benefit recitals should be the product of careful research and should be as site-specific as possible. This is not only because in them the grantors suggest their case for meeting the conservation purpose test for the deductibility of their easement donation under federal and state tax laws (a case for which they should be able to provide detailed supporting evidence if questioned) but also because they provide a public policy rationale for enforcing the easement that will assist the courts in any future dispute over its terms. Historically, American law has not favored long-term private restrictions on the exercise of property rights and has devised numerous mechanisms for removing them. In the years to come, conservation easements are likely to stand or fall on the strength of their identification with the public interest—the premise on which the statutory authority for conservation easements, now established in all but a few states, is built.[2]

Sample Qualitative Description Recitals

The following paragraphs, loosely adapted from sample conservation easement forms prepared by the Maine Coast Heritage Trust for its coastal island resource protection program, illustrate the approach in the context of a hypothetical island property that exhibits both natural (the first seven paragraphs) and scenic (the last three paragraphs) qualities of substantial significance:

...WHEREAS, in particular, the Maine coast, and that portion of the Maine coast in which the Property is located known as the Five Bay tidal region, is a relatively intact coastal ecosystem and, as such, provides important habitat for a wide variety of birds, fishes, and both marine and terrestrial mammals and plants; and

WHEREAS, the Property, which exists in a substantially undisturbed natural state, harbors a diversity of plant and animal life in an unusually broad range of habitats for a property of its size, including a cobble barrier beach and associated wetlands, nesting ledges, a spruce fir forest, and open meadows, the locations of which are indicated in Exhibit ____ attached hereto and incorporated by this reference; and

WHEREAS, the Five Bay tidal region is an active nesting territory for the endangered bald eagle as documented by the United States Fish and Wildlife Service, *An Ecological Characterization of Coastal Maine*, FWS/OBS-80/29 (October 1980); and

WHEREAS, a bald eagle nesting site is located on the Property as indicated in Exhibit ____, which site has been identified, surveyed, and documented as nest site 20C by the Maine Eagle Project, a project of the Maine Department of Inland Fisheries and Wildlife and the Wildlife Division, College of Natural Resources, University of Maine at Orono, under agreement with the U.S. Fish and Wildlife Service; and

---

2. As the conservation easement concept has taken hold, the notion of public benefit that is at its core has been applied in at least one jurisdiction to uphold an easement that would have been unenforceable under earlier common law principles. *See Bennett v. Commissioner of Food and Agriculture*, 411 Mass. 1, 576 N.E.2d 1365 (1991).

WHEREAS, the Property lies in close proximity to Eagle Island, Little Mar Island, and Whale Rock, all of which are in public ownership by either the Maine Department of Inland Fisheries and Wildlife or the Maine Bureau of Public Lands and which contain nesting sites for a diversity of coastal waterbirds, including black guillemots, common eiders, common terns, least terns, and double-crested cormorants, as documented by the United States Fish and Wildlife Service, Biological Services Program, *Coastal Waterbird Colonies* (1977); and

WHEREAS, because of the integrated nature of the coastal ecosystem, the use made of the Property will affect not only the conservation values of the Property but those of these and other neighboring islands as well; and

WHEREAS, in recognition of the importance of the Property as an ecological and scenic resource, a major portion of the Property, as indicated in Exhibit ____, has been designated a Critical Area by the State of Maine in the Register of Maine Critical Areas and the entire property is classified by the same registry as a scenic coastal island; and

WHEREAS, the town of Big Bay in its comprehensive plan has designated the area where the Property is located as a Scenic Coastal District; and

WHEREAS, the Property is situated on and prominently visible from the public waterways of Long Sound, which sustain substantial recreational boating traffic; and...

Two further examples of public benefit recitals, one from an agricultural open space easement, the other involving outdoor recreation, help to round out the picture.

An agricultural open space easement will typically describe the quality of the property's soils. The following example is adapted from an easement prepared by the Land Trust for Santa Barbara County:

...WHEREAS, the Property, which has a long history of productive ranching and farming, contains significant areas with soil classifications designated as Srf (Shedd silty clay loam), SdA and SdC (Salinas silty clay loam) and has been identified by the Natural Resource Conservation Service of the U. S. Department of Agriculture as farmland of statewide and local importance in accordance with the classification standards of that agency; and...

A recreational component might be as simple as a trail network link-up. This example is also adapted from a Land Trust for Santa Barbara County easement:

...WHEREAS, the installation and maintenance of a trail through the woodland area will assist in the completion of the _____ District's public trail system and provide an important opportunity for public recreation on the Property, including hiking, bicycling, horseback riding, and nature study; and...

Examples could be multiplied, of course, all of which, needless to say, would be entirely fact dependent, but these make the point. The important thing, for drafting purposes, is that the qualitative description recitals lay out the specific conservation values of the property in question with sufficient detail to provide both a factual context and a public policy rationale for the use restrictions to follow.

7. Baseline Documentation

The IRS requires a donor who retains rights in the property whose exercise could impair the property's conservation values to provide documentation prior to the grant "sufficient to establish the condition of the property at the time of the gift," including the condition of any resources, such as soil and water, specifically identified for protection. Both parties must acknowledge in a signed statement accompanying the baseline documentation that the documentation accurately represents the condition of the property at the time of the transfer. *See* Treas. Reg. § 1.170A-14(g)(5)(i).

There is no requirement that the documentation be made part of the easement itself. It is important, however, as a practical matter, that the relationship of this material to the easement be made clear in the easement, since its function is to provide the grantee with a starting point for monitoring the grantor's compliance with the terms of the easement. Some practitioners attach the baseline documentation to, and record it with, the easement. Rules governing the recordation of photographs, overlays, and other graphic material that is not of standard size or quality vary from jurisdiction to jurisdiction. In some states, this material may not all be recordable. If the baseline documentation is not to be recorded, it should be incorporated by reference and grantee's custodianship noted. In most jurisdictions, assuming the documentation is where it is represented to be, this is sufficient to put subsequent purchasers and encumbrancers on notice of its contents to the same extent as if it were recorded.

The use of formal baseline documentation in support of a conservation easement is a relatively new development. Were it not for the 1986 IRS requirements, it is unlikely the practice would have become pervasive among land trusts and other conservation grantees for some time to come. There is no doubt that carefully prepared baseline material can be a considerable aid to monitoring and enforcing a grantor's performance of an easement's terms. Easement drafters should be careful, however, not to become too dependent on it. Good baseline documentation presents a "snapshot" of the property at the time of the grant, but even if it were possible, the purpose of an easement is not to freeze the land at one moment in time. With limited exceptions (as when affirmative maintenance obligations or rights are involved—to preserve a meadow against forest encroachment, for example), an easement is not intended to interrupt the cycles of change on the land but rather to restrict, to varying degrees, a landowner's freedom to interfere with those cycles.

Consequently, given the dynamic nature of land and the subtlety and complexity of the forces that effect changes in it, "the condition of the property at the time of the gift" is likely to become a decreasingly useful reference point over the long haul. For this reason among others (the baseline documentation, if not recorded, could be lost, damaged, or destroyed, and whether recorded or not, it could prove to be a less than perfect, or even wholly inadequate, reference source in some cases), a drafter should approach the task of drafting an easement as if there were to be no supporting documentation. All that is necessary to understand and enforce the easement should be contained within the four corners of the easement instrument. Although the baseline documentation, ideally, will provide useful evidence of the conservation values of a property, typically it will not be considered the exclusive source of evidence, and in any case, it should not be necessary to look beyond the easement itself to identify what those values are.

The utility of the baseline data is extended by the updating provided by monitoring reports, which are the product of a grantee's regular inspections of the property. In situations where the baseline data is to be recorded, it is the practice of some drafters to provide an express right in the Grantee to record the product of its monitoring efforts as well, to serve as supplementary baseline documentation, when appropriate.

The IRS regulations give a useful catalogue of what the baseline documentation might include. *See* Treas. Reg. § 1.170A-14(g)(5)(i). Whether baseline documentation is required at all and if so how detailed it should be are questions that can be answered only on a case-by-case basis. The variables include the potential for conflict that exists between a grantor's reserved rights and the conservation resources to be protected as well as the sensitivity and complexity of those resources.

8. Continuation of Existing Uses

The intention to permit the existing uses of the property to continue is made clear. A qualifier might be added, as appropriate, to indicate that these uses are to be undertaken in conformity with an approved management plan or other performance standards set forth elsewhere in the easement.

9. Conveyance of Right to Protect Conservation Values: Affirmative Purpose

Although most people think of conservation easements as essentially negative in character because of the many restrictions on land use they typically contain, it may be useful, conceptually, to remember that, in the usual case (buffer-type easements are an exception), the restrictions in an easement are in support of an overarching affirmative purpose to see to the preservation of the conservation values of the restricted property itself. This affirmative purpose distinguishes the typical conservation easement from traditional negative easements, covenants, and servitudes, whose primary purpose is in some way to enhance or protect the value of property *outside* the boundaries of the property subject to them.

Enabling legislation in most states has made speculation regarding the nature of a conservation easement a matter of little more than theoretical interest. It is at least conceivable, however, that in states that have not enacted such legislation, this technical distinction could have a bearing on the enforceability of the "novel" conservation easement, particularly in light of the fact that the courts have been reluctant, traditionally, to expand the exceedingly narrow category of negative easements that are considered valid under the common law. Arguably, a right to protect certain features of a property is no less "affirmative," conceptually, than a right-of-way across it and should be no less enforceable. In any case, emphasizing this affirmative aspect of the easement is a subtle way of encouraging the parties to think of the conservation values it protects as something as real and positive, in their way, as the development rights it restricts.

10. Qualifications of Grantee

The grantee must be shown to meet all state and federal qualifying requirements relevant to the easement transaction in question. This paragraph (including the bracketed portion) tracks the language of one state's enabling statute almost word for word, with the addition of the clause stating the grantee's qualification under Section 170(h) of the Internal Revenue Code. The federal tax regulations require that a grantee have both the commitment and resources to enforce the easement. *See* Treas. Reg. § 1.170A-14(c)(1). An organization "organized or operated primarily or substantially" for a qualified conservation purpose meets the commitment test automatically. Whether the organization's resources are sufficient is a separate question of fact, but a dedicated monitoring fund is expressly not required. This recital marks the end of the preamble.

11. Grant

This formal clause is, from a property lawyer's perspective, where the real business of the easement begins, because it is here that the transfer of the property interest is effected. Care must be taken to use language that complies with the conveyancing requirements of the jurisdiction in which the subject property is located, which in some cases may mean strict adherence to seemingly archaic formulae. One variable is the way in which consideration is recited. In some states a nominal dollar amount (for example, $10.00) is customarily stated to have changed hands; in others, explicit gift, sale, or bargain sale language is used depending on the circumstances of the transaction. Although discussion of the issue is beyond the scope of this commentary, it is to be noted that, under certain circumstances, the common law favors transfers for consideration over gift transfers. The model follows the modern practice, which is broadly if not universally accepted, of reciting that it is the exchange of promises contained in the agreement that provides the consideration for the grant.

Where there is statutory authority for the easement, and in some states more than one statute may apply, this authority should be invoked to ensure that the easement will benefit from it in the event of a challenge. Of course, state easement statutes may impose certain conveyancing requirements of their own, and in the model the grantors are characterized as "voluntarily" making the grant to comply with a requirement to that effect in one such statute. That the grant be made "in perpetuity" is a statutory requirement in some states as it is under Section 170(h) of the Internal Revenue Code.

In addition to whatever statutory authority may exist, some practitioners invoke the common law, presumably as insurance against the failure of the easement to meet statutory requirements or the failure of the supporting statutes themselves. In light of the fact that the common law authority for conservation easements has never been established, this does not seem to be a particularly helpful practice. Out of caution for the concerns just raised, the model makes general reference to the law of the state where the property is located in addition to the specific statutory authority. Whether the courts will enforce a conservation easement without specific statutory authority, however, is an open question.[3]

As discussed in **comment 4 (Title Representation and Legal Description of the Property)**, it is common practice in states without conservation easement enabling legislation to carve a small parcel out of the property and convey it in fee to the grantee along with the easement in order to circumvent common law limitations on the enforceability of negative easements in gross (*i.e.*, not running to the benefit of another property). The easement may then be described as "appurtenant" to the parcel conveyed in fee. Typically, the fee parcel will be transferred to the grantee subject to deed restrictions, reservations, or a cross-easement allowing the grantor to continue to use the parcel while assuring its use will be consistent with the restrictions imposed on the larger parcel. The following example, adapted from a form developed by the Jackson Hole Land Trust, illustrates the approach:

> NOW, THEREFORE, in consideration of the above and the mutual covenants, terms, conditions, and restrictions contained herein:
>
> A. Grantor hereby grants and conveys to Grantee that portion of the Property described in Exhibit ____ (the "Trust Parcel"), excepting and reserving with respect to the Trust Parcel, a conservation easement, as hereinafter defined (the "Retained Easement"), to preserve and protect the conservation values of the Trust Parcel, together with the right to enter upon and use the

---

3. For a discussion of the common law problems that have led to a statutory solution in most states, see the Uniform Conservation Easement Act, 12 U.L.A. 51 (Supp. 1986). *See also* Andrew Dana and Michael Ramsey, *Conservation Easements and the Common Law*, 8 Stan. Env. L.J. 1, (1989); Thomas S. Barrett and Putnam Livermore, *The Conservation Easement in California* 27-28, 113-118 (Island Press 1983). The author is aware of one instance where a hostile landowner has attempted to use a common law reference to invalidate an easement. On the other hand, in jurisdictions where the common law is evolving to accommodate conservation easements (*see, e.g., Bennett v. Commissioner of Food and Agriculture*, 411 Mass. 1, 576 N.E.2d 1365 (1991)), such a reference might prove useful.

Trust Parcel for all purposes authorized under the terms of Paragraphs 3 and 4 [Prohibited Uses and Reserved Rights] below. The Retained Easement and other rights of entry and use reserved by Grantor with respect to the Trust Parcel shall be appurtenant to that portion of the Property described in Exhibit ___ (the "Principal Property") and shall benefit and be enforceable by Grantor in perpetuity.

B. Grantor hereby voluntarily grants and conveys to Grantee a conservation easement, as hereinafter defined (the "Principal Easement"), over and across all the Principal Property to preserve and protect the conservation values of the Property, which Principal Easement shall be appurtenant to the Trust Parcel and shall benefit and be enforceable by Grantee and shall bind Grantor in perpetuity.

Use of the term "grant" in a deed implies in most jurisdictions that the grantor has not previously conveyed or encumbered the interest being transferred. In addition, a grantor may agree to give title warranties to insure the grantee against defects in the title to the interest conveyed. Depending on the formal requirements of the jurisdiction involved, the grant might then read: "Grantors hereby voluntarily grant, convey, *and warrant* to Grantee a conservation easement..."; or "Grantors hereby grant to Grantee *with warranty covenants* a conservation easement..."—to give two examples. Warranties may be expressly limited to encumbrances "not of sight or record" (*i.e.*, apparent upon physical inspection or search of the record) at the time the easement is executed. Whether or not title warranties are given, the grantee should satisfy itself as to the condition of title by searching the title record down to the date of closing. Title insurance might also be obtained.

Some easements, reaching beyond the standard approach illustrated by the model are designed not only to restrict development of a property but to transfer any severable development rights that may accrue to the property under local zoning laws or transferable development rights programs. This approach is discussed under "development rights" in **comment 15 (Prohibited Uses: Express Restrictions)**.

12. Purpose (paragraph 1)

Although it appears on first reading to be nothing more than an innocuous recapitulation of the recitals, the purpose clause is, in fact, the touchstone of the easement. Everything turns on the "consistency" test that is introduced here. Only uses that are not inconsistent with protection of the conservation values of the property are now permitted. In the provisions to follow, the parties' judgment concerning the consistency of specific uses will be made express. So, for example, farming, ranching, or timber production, with or without qualification as appropriate, may be permitted, while residential and commercial development, additional construction, and mining may be prohibited or restricted. It is likely to be impossible, however, to foresee every conceivable future use or variation of use.

Unless the parties intend that either the specific restrictions imposed or the grantor's expressly reserved rights are to be exclusive, there must be some mechanism for dealing with the unforeseen. The consistency test is that mechanism. If the easement is reasonably clear about the conservation values to be protected, it should provide a workable standard.

It should be noted that in this paragraph, as elsewhere, the choice of language is influenced by relevant statutory and regulatory provisions. Stating the purpose of the easement to be, in part, the retention of land "predominantly" in its, for example, natural, scenic, or open space condition is to key into a state enabling statute (caveat: the appropriate language will vary from state to state). Reference to preventing uses of the property that "significantly impair or interfere with conservation values" echoes similar language in the IRS regulations. See Treas. Reg. § § 1.170A-14(d)(4)(v), (e)(2), (g)(4), and (g)(5). Some practitioners, concerned that the qualifier "significantly" is too vague, prefer to leave it out. Others consider it a buffer against the tension that might exist in a multipurpose open space easement between the desire to preserve a given land use, like farming, and the desire to protect other values, like wildlife, as well.

Where conflict between values is potentially significant, it is important that the primary purpose of an easement be clearly identified and other potentially conflicting values or uses made expressly subordinate to it, if at all possible. See Treas. Reg. § 1.170A-14(e)(2)-(3).[4] This is easier to do when the values of a given property lend themselves to being "zoned" in an easement—into a "farmland area" and a "natural preservation area," for example. The purpose section of a New Jersey Conservation Foundation multipurpose easement, as adapted below, reflects this zoned approach:

Purpose. It is the purpose of this Easement that:

(a) The portion of the Property more particularly described in Exhibit B (the "Farmland Area") be forever retained and preserved as open-field farmland, wetlands, and mature woodland for agricultural and natural resource conservation uses and be utilized in a manner which conserves the quality of the soils for open-field agricultural use;

(b) the portion of the Property more particularly described in Exhibit C (the "Natural Preservation Area") be forever preserved and protected in its natural state for natural resource conservation uses and free from all agricultural, residential, and commercial uses of any kind and from all activities that might damage, compromise or interfere with its ecological diversity, natural beauty, and resource quality or with the natural processes occurring therein; and

---

4. See also discussion in Stephen J. Small, *The Federal Tax Law of Conservation Easements* 12-2 to 12-3 (Land Trust Alliance 1986).

(c) the portion of the Property more particularly described in Exhibit D (the "Pathway Area") be preserved and protected in the same manner and for the same purposes as the Natural Preservation Area, except for the right of the public to use it for purposes of a public walkway with improvements ancillary thereto.

Grantor intends that this Easement will confine the use of the Property to such activities as are not inconsistent with the purpose of this Easement.

In a helpful definitions section immediately following the purpose clause, the New Jersey Conservation Foundation easement goes on to state that the defined conservation, as opposed to agricultural, values of the property, paramount in the "Natural Preservation Area" and the "Pathway Area," are subordinate within the designated "Farmland Area" if they should "specifically conflict with the Grantor's use of the Farmland Area for the agricultural purposes contemplated herein." Use of the Farmland Area, however, must be in accordance with an agreed upon "Management Plan."

In jurisdictions where recitals are considered to have no substantive legal effect, the important explanatory contents of the recitals should be shifted to the purpose clause, or the recitals should be incorporated here by reference. If the latter course is chosen, an introductory incorporating clause might read:

It is the purpose of this Easement to implement the mutual intentions of the parties as expressed in the above recitals, which are incorporated here by this reference, and in the provisions that follow, by assuring that the Property will be retained forever...etc.

13. Rights of Grantee (paragraph 2)

The scope of the rights conveyed to the grantee depends on the type of easement in question. Recreational or educational easements, for example, might contain highly detailed descriptions of permitted activities, circumscribed by specific conditions and qualifications and confined to precisely delineated time periods. Natural ecosystem easements, on the other hand, might delegate broad authority to the grantee to manage or maintain the property and to make its own determination regarding limitations on access. The greater the degree of public access or the greater the degree of management control conveyed by an easement, of course, the greater a grantee's potential exposure to personal injury or hazardous materials liability, an issue that is discussed in **comment 26 (Representations, Warranties, and Remediation)** and **comment 27 (Hold Harmless)**. Not uncommonly, only modest ancillary rights are desired, such as, depending on the circumstances, a right to conduct scientific or educational studies or observations and to perform limited sampling, or rights to post signs, conduct tours, maintain trails, and the like.

The model provides the essentials, giving the grantee the broad power to protect the conservation values of the property but confining the grantee's supporting rights to those that are necessary for proper monitoring and enforcement of the easement (inspection, injunctive relief, and restoration). Recognizing that the typical open space easement is over property that is being put to some productive use by its owners, the model requires that the grantee's rights be exercised without undue interference with the landowner's use and quiet enjoyment of the property. ("Quiet enjoyment" is a legal term of art connoting freedom from outside disturbance; of course, the landowner's own use of the property can be as *noisy* as the easement, local ordinances, or other applicable laws or regulations otherwise permit.) Conveyance of the rights of inspection, enforcement, and restoration is dictated not only by common sense but by the IRS. *See* Treas. Reg. § 1.170A-14(g)(5)(ii). If the parties so desire, the permitted frequency of inspection and the length of the required notice period can be specified, though some recognition of possible emergency circumstances seems only prudent. Some grantors may insist that the grantee's right of entry be exercised at its own risk.

The continuing right to "identify" the conservation values of the property is sometimes conveyed, particularly in natural ecosystem easements. In the typical open space easement, however, the conservation values are identified up front, and it would be an impermissible enlargement of the burden of the easement to unilaterally identify new values after the conveyance. Depending on the circumstances, too much open-endedness can also leave the easement vulnerable to attack on grounds of vagueness.

A grantee may desire the right to make scientific studies of the conservation values of the property. If so, care should be taken to carefully delimit the scope of the right in order to allay any concerns a grantor might have that it could become too intrusive. Finally, under certain circumstances the parties may contemplate engaging in specific projects to restore or enhance the conservation values of the property. If so, a right of enhancement should be included to prevent a change of ownership from undercutting the planned projects.

Some practitioners seek to further empower the grantee, in its sole discretion, to determine the consistency of any activity or use, for which no express provision is made, with the purpose of the easement or the protection of particular resources. Where an acquisition is by purchase as opposed to donation, or where a natural ecosystem is involved, the point may be pressed with particular force. This is a potentially powerful enforcement tool, should questions about the suitability of unanticipated activities or uses arise in the future, and is well worth pursuing. Typically, however, the grantor will wish to preserve a say in the matter. In the model, the issue is left open to negotiation and, if necessary, mediation or arbitration (see alternate paragraphs 5.3 of the supplementary provisions) or litigation through the grantee's exercise of the section 6 remedies referred to in subparagraph 2(c).

14. Prohibited Uses (paragraph 3)

There are three basic approaches to structuring the restrictive provisions of a conservation easement. The first is to make the restrictions exclusive; anything not expressly prohibited is permitted. This approach is seen most frequently in simple, single purpose easements, such as the "pothole" easements taken by the U.S. Fish and Wildlife Service to protect the wetlands along the migratory waterfowl flyway of the upper Great Plains. In the pothole easements the draining, filling, leveling, or burning of wetlands is prohibited, but no other obligations or restrictions are imposed, and all other rights are reserved to the grantors.

The second approach is to delineate the specific rights retained by the grantor and convey all other rights to the grantee. This approach—which it is more accurate to characterize as the grant of a fee subject to reserved rights than a grant of a conservation easement—has been preferred in recent years by federal agencies.[5] The intention behind "reserved interest deeds," as they are called, is to make enforcement easier. Although as yet untested, they presume to shift the burden of proof on matters regarding which the deed is silent or unclear from the grantee to the grantor. Reserved interest deeds have been acquired by the National Park Service along the Appalachian Trail and by the Forest Service at the Oregon Dune National Recreation Area and Columbia Gorge National Scenic Area—presumably at a premium above the standard price for conservation easements. Among the questions they raise is the extent to which liabilities incumbent on land ownership—such as, for example, property tax or CERCLA liability—are transferred with the grant. Their status under state laws relating to conservation easements may vary from state to state.

An advantage of both these approaches—exclusive restrictions or exclusive reservations—is their apparent certainty; they are meant to leave little doubt as to the scope of the interest conveyed. But, as always, there is a cost. By fixing the terms of either the restrictions or reservations, these instruments allocate the risk of an omission entirely to one party or the other. In a complicated setting, where conservation concerns and productive uses require careful balancing in perpetuity, a one-way allocation of risk may be too inflexible and therefore unacceptable. Not surprisingly, the third approach, which the model adopts, and which is found in one variation or another in most of the easements reviewed for this commentary, follows a middle course. It prohibits all uses that are inconsistent with the purpose of the easement and reserves to the grantor the right to engage in all uses that are not inconsistent.

The restrictions and reservations of an early two-acre "forever wild" easement, quoted in their entirety, illustrate the third approach in its simplest form:

> The Premises shall be kept as open space in their natural and wild state and restricted from any development with buildings or otherwise, or any use other than as open space and as sanctuary for wildlife and wild plants.
>
> It is understood, however, that the Conservation Easement herein granted

---

5. *See* U.S. Department of the Interior, National Park Service, Office of Park Planning and Special Studies, *Planning Process Guideline,* Release No. 3, Amendment No. 3, 4-5 and 38-42 (March 1986); *see also* James Snow, *Reserved Interest Deeds: An Alternate Approach to Drafting Conservation Easements,* The Back Forty, February 1992, at 1, and accompanying commentary.

permits the Grantors and their successors in interest to use the Premises for all purposes, present and future, not inconsistent with this grant.

While these paragraphs can hardly be considered adequate by today's drafting standards, the emphasis they place on the purpose of the easement—which, as discussed in **comment 12 (Purpose)**, is the touchstone of the instrument—is instructive. It puts the focus where ultimately it has to be for a document intended to reach so far into the unknowable future.

As experience with easements has grown and unexpected problems have been encountered and overcome, easement practice has become, inevitably, more sophisticated. Today's easement drafters often go to great lengths to anticipate future problems and to provide for them expressly in the easement deed. Particularly where conservation values and productive uses are intermingled, it is not uncommon to find highly detailed restrictions and reservations—in some cases, in fact, so detailed that they begin to resemble zoning code provisions. The intention is to create a document that leaves as little room for interpretation as possible, one whose terms can be applied almost mechanically. Enforceability and, in the case of a deductible easement gift, an accurate, defensible appraisal are motivating goals.

But there are limits to the benefits of specificity. Too much detail can alienate the landowner, whose willing cooperation is, as a practical matter, integral to the success of an easement. And, in any case, time has a way of rendering details obsolete. A document conceived for perpetuity must have stretch; it must have application to changing conditions—the unforeseen as well as the foreseen.

Most practitioners, recognizing the futility of trying to delimit every conceivable variation of use, activity, or practice that in the future might have an adverse impact on the resources to be protected, build in some flexibility. As in the simple easement quoted above, most easements provide that consistency with the purpose of the easement is the standard that all future actions must meet, whether dealt with expressly in the easement instrument or not. If the purpose of the easement is carefully articulated and the conservation values of the property clearly identified—and if the relationship of the specific restrictions to these values is clear—the consistency catch-all should serve to prevent the easement from being defeated for lack of clairvoyance on the part of its drafter. This is not to say that distinguishing between what is consistent and inconsistent with the purpose of an easement will always be easy. Seasoned practitioners know better. But at least the consistency mechanism should serve to keep the question on the table.[6]

15. Prohibited Uses: Express Restrictions (paragraph 3)

The content of an easement's restrictive provisions is, of course, entirely dependent on the facts at hand and must be thought through on a case-by-case

---

6. *See* Robert J. Sugarman, *Legal Challenges to Conservation Easements: The French and Pickering Creeks Conservation Trust Experience,* The Back Forty, January-February 1992, at 9, for a description of a successful easement defense based on just these principles.

basis. The requirements of natural ecosystem, recreational, educational, scenic, open space, farm, forest, and multipurpose easements differ, often markedly, from one another. In addition, the requirements of particular easements within a given class are as varied as the properties to which they apply, the regions of the country in which they are located, and the practical needs and temperaments of the parties who negotiate them. Seemingly infinite permutations are possible. Nevertheless, one can speak in a general way of certain basic areas of concern that are likely to come up more often than not. Restrictions regarding the following uses and resources seem to recur with the greatest frequency:

- subdivision and development
- commercial or industrial use
- new and existing buildings, structures, roads, and other improvements
- alteration of the land surface
- mineral development
- waste dumps
- utility lines
- signs
- soil and water
- wetlands
- ponds and streams
- wildlife and wildlife habitat
- trees, shrubs, and other vegetation

The degree of control imposed by an easement to regulate these uses and resources is highly variable and depends, among other things, on the conservation values identified for protection. And, of course, depending on the type of easement involved, other concerns may require attention. An agricultural easement, for example, may require conformity with a farm conservation plan prepared by the district conservationist of the Natural Resource Conservation Service (formerly the Soil Conservation Service), or may go beyond that and impose specific restrictions on farming practices to protect streams, control runoff and erosion, limit the use of pesticides, and enhance soil quality. Similarly, a timberland easement is likely to impose restrictions aimed at protecting the forest resource by requiring an approved plan, by making reference to some generally accepted performance standards, or by setting forth specific requirements. Scenic easements may have provisions for maintaining open fields and meadows, preventing the obstruction of a view, and limiting parking areas. Natural habitat easements may seek to protect native vegetation from non-native encroachment and to limit hunting, fishing, or trapping. The list can be extended indefinitely, but it has little meaning in the abstract. The circumstances of a particular transaction, and the facts on the ground, are always controlling.[7]

---

7. A helpful discussion of typical restrictive provisions, by category, can be found in National Trust for Historic Preservation and the Land Trust Alliance, *Appraising Easements: Guidelines for Valuation of Historic Preservation and Land Conservation Easements* (1991). *See also* Barrett and Livermore, *The Conservation Easement in California* 86-91.

Because the content of the restrictive provisions is entirely fact-based, the best a model can do is give some general guidance on how these provisions should be approached. There are two major concerns: balance and coherence. As to the first, which runs to policy, the grantee should be at pains to intrude no further on the landowner's beneficial use and enjoyment of the property than the protection of the conservation values of the property requires. Pride of ownership runs deep; landowners, rightly, value their prerogatives. As a general rule, grantees should not use easements to impose their own preferences in inessential matters like taste or, unless the easement is part of a comprehensive regional protection plan, to try to solve problems that transcend the boundaries of the property. The grantee should stick to restrictions that will make a substantial difference to the conservation values of the property, that it can monitor efficiently, and that it intends to enforce.

In addition, an effort should be made to scale the grantee's degree of control over the landowner's activities in a manner that corresponds to the severity of the threat the activities pose to the conservation values of the property. Fully compatible uses can be permitted without restriction; fully incompatible uses should be prohibited outright. In between, recognized performance standards, notice requirements, or approval requirements can be used, in escalating order, to prevent or mitigate conflicts. The more sensitive the resource to be protected, of course, the tighter the controls, but the grantee should make every effort to understand the resource, determine its tolerance to use, and give as much latitude for permitted uses, including economic uses, as possible. The less burdensome an easement's requirements, the less occasion there will be for conflict and the easier in the long run the easement will be to enforce. Particularly in the context of farm, forest, or other open space preservation, where the parties envision the coexistence of conservation values and one or more intensive productive uses, the less the landowner and the easement holder have to think about the easement in everyday situations the better.

The second concern, coherence, is a mechanical matter. The pieces of an easement should all fit together. Restrictions and permitted uses and activities should not be in conflict. Interrelationships between them should be identified, and cross-references made where appropriate. The restrictions should be presented in some logical sequence and related subjects grouped. Overly vague or ambiguous terms should be avoided. In addition, exhibits should be used as necessary to describe the location of a protected resource or permitted use.

One final note: in the restrictions, as throughout the easement, care must be taken to include any provisions required by applicable state law. Certain specific restrictions or permitted uses might be required, for example, to qualify under a state or local program for preferential property tax treatment, as is sometimes accorded certain lands devoted to agriculture, timber production, or other open space land uses.

Sample Restrictions

The following necessarily generic provisions show a few variations on the theme. Individually, they are meant to mimic the kinds of provisions one might find in a typical open space easement, but it is important to understand that the parts cannot be summed into a whole. Natural, scenic, forest, and farmland elements are combined in them for purposes of illustration, but they have been assembled in a vacuum. Real negotiations over a real piece of property would almost certainly lead to a far different balancing of concerns. As experienced hands know, there can be no such thing as a consensus set of easement restrictions: what is right on one set of facts is likely to be wrong on another. Consequently, the reader is cautioned to bear in mind that these sample restrictions are offered not for their substance but for whatever limited guidance they might give as to form.

It should be noted that these restrictions will be fully comprehensible only if read in light of the reserved rights discussed in **comments 16 and 17**. Reference to paragraph 4 in these provisions should be read as reference to the reserved rights. As a matter of convenience, comments on particular provisions are interspersed.

Development, Subdivision, Construction

SUBDIVISION

(a) The legal or *de facto* division, subdivision, or partitioning of the Property for any purpose, except as may be required by law for the uses permitted in subparagraph 3(d);...

Carving up a property into multiple, separately saleable parcels through subdivision or otherwise—a necessary precondition for intensive residential as well as many other kinds of development—is the primary threat to open space. It is safe to say that the principal objective of most easements is to prohibit or control it, and in the usual case, this one provision accounts for virtually the entire diminution of market value caused by an easement.

Where limited development is contemplated, the easement should delineate the areas in which it is permitted if they have not been excluded from the easement altogether. Where the property under easement is already divided into more than one parcel, some easements prohibit their separate conveyance, which, among other things, makes the easement easier to administer, monitor, and enforce. On the grounds that division of the property need not be detrimental in all cases, however, some practitioners leave an opening for it with the grantee's prior approval.

The exception to the prohibition of this paragraph refers to the provision dealing with permitted construction and improvements, which is discussed below. Some jurisdictions require legal subdivision for the construction of even one additional dwelling.

Normally, the conveyance or bequest of an undivided interest in the entire property would not be prohibited under the terms of this provision. Both practically and legally the enforceability of such a prohibition might prove problematic. If a limitation is intended on leases, licenses, and the like, it should be made explicit.

DEVELOPMENT RIGHTS

(b) The use, exercise, or transfer of development rights on or to the Property, or any portion thereof, as it is now or hereafter may be bounded or described, or any other property within the _____ District described in Exhibit ___, except as may be required by law for the uses permitted in subparagraph 3(d). For the purposes of this subparagraph, "development rights" include, without limitation, any and all rights, however designated, now or hereafter associated with the Property or any other property that may be used, pursuant to applicable zoning laws or other governmental laws or regulations, to compute permitted size, height, bulk, or number of structures, development density, lot yield, or any similar development variable on or pertaining to the Property or any other property;...

An important issue that has been gaining increased attention in recent years is the relationship of the conservation easement to transferable development rights created by state or local law. Transferable development rights programs, which create a market mechanism for the transfer of development rights from low to high density areas, are being used with increasing frequency across the country to moderate the inequities inherent in zoning decisions.[8]

Of related and even more immediate concern to holders of conservation easements is cluster zoning. Cluster zoning, a now quite common land use planning technique, might be described as a transfer of development rights within a single parcel of land or between adjacent parcels under common ownership. Unlike the off-site impacts of TDRs, however, the impacts of cluster zoning are likely to be felt directly by a protected parcel.

Although related by their subject matter, easements and transferable development rights or credits are not necessarily mutually exclusive. An easement is not, properly speaking, a conveyance or even an extinguishment of development rights but rather a conveyance of, among other things, the right to prevent or restrict development on a particular parcel of land. Created by statute or ordinance, transferable development rights constitute an additional, entirely distinct property interest.

Theoretically, the jurisdiction instituting a transferable development rights or cluster zoning program can, if it so chooses, recognize an entitlement to such rights without in any way impinging on an easement over the property involved. From a property law perspective, an easement holder should have no claim on such rights merely as a consequence of its easement interest.[9] Presumably, though, both with respect to TDRs and cluster zoning, the parties to an easement

---

8. County or regional programs exist in many states, including California, Florida, Maryland, and New Jersey. *See Expanding Land Trusts' Conservation Efforts Through Involvement in TDR Programs,* The Back Forty, January-February 1993, at 13.

9. *See Friends of the Shawangunks, Inc. v. Knowlton,* 64 N.Y.2d 387, 476 N.E.2d 988 (1985), where the existence of a conservation easement over one portion of a property did not preclude counting the burdened acreage in calculating the increased density to be permitted on the remainder of the property under a local cluster zoning ordinance.

are free to bargain for whatever allocation or restriction of these rights they consider appropriate.[10] And predictably, provisions clarifying the parties' interests are beginning to find their way into easements in jurisdictions where cluster zoning or transferable development rights are a factor. While the approaches taken vary, the primary concern is to assure that any exercise of these rights not adversely affect the conservation values of the property under easement.

One approach, as in the sample, is to restrict or prohibit the exercise of residual development rights on or near the property. Where an easement covers only a portion of a given property, a cluster zoning ordinance might permit the allocation of development rights or credits from the burdened open space to adjacent or nearby areas of the property that are not under easement.[11] While an easement over the entire property would normally foreclose this possibility, it would not prevent a development rights transfer to an adjacent or nearby property that might adversely impact the easement and even, perhaps, a regional conservation project of which the easement represents only one piece. The sample assumes, for purposes of illustration, an easement that burdens only a portion of a given property and is drafted to prevent transfers both within and without the boundaries of the property.

Another approach, more comprehensive than a restriction, would be the outright conveyance of development rights to the grantee, with or without an expression of intent to extinguish them. Practitioners should be aware, however, that the ability of the parties to convey or extinguish rights that may not yet exist under local law could be open to question. If a conveyance is intended, language similar to the following might be added to the grant clause:

> ...Grantors hereby voluntarily grant and convey to Grantee a conservation easement in perpetuity over the Property, *together with all unreserved development rights associated with the Property*, of the nature and character and to the extent hereinafter set forth ("Easement").

The "Rights of Grantee" provision might then be expanded to describe the scope of the development rights conveyed, in terms similar to the following:

> (d) Any and all development rights now or hereafter associated with the Property, including, without limitation, all rights, however designated, that may be used pursuant to applicable zoning laws, or other governmental laws or regulations, to compute permitted size, height, bulk, or number of structures, development density, lot yield, or any similar development variable on or pertaining to the Property or any other property, except those reserved under paragraph 4. [The parties agree that the development rights so

---

10. *See* Scott Ferguson, *Easement Drafting: Addressing the Possibility of Transferable Development Rights,* The Back Forty, July/August 1994, at 7; *see also* William R. Ginsberg, *Will a Conservation Easement Extinguish Development Rights?,* LTA Exchange, Spring 1993, at 13.

11. This was the case in *Friends of the Shawangunks v. Knowlton,* 64 N.Y.2d 387, 476 N.E.2d 988 (1985).

conveyed {are hereby terminated and extinguished and} may not be used on or transferred to any portion of the Property as it is now or hereafter may be bounded or described, {or to any property within the _____ District described in Exhibit ___ -or- or to any other property adjacent or otherwise}. {Grantors agree to cooperate fully with Grantee in any application by Grantee to use, sell, or otherwise benefit from such development rights and shall execute and deliver any consents or other documents as may be necessary for such purposes or to otherwise assist Grantee in perfecting its rights under this subparagraph.}]

As the sample indicates, any development rights required to be allocated for any permitted construction on the property should be expressly reserved.

A final point to bear in mind is that, depending on the circumstances, how development rights are handled could very well affect the valuation of an easement for tax purposes.[12]

COMMERCIAL DEVELOPMENT

(c) Any commercial or industrial use of or activity on the Property other than those relating to agriculture, recreation, or home occupations as permitted under paragraph 4 or mineral development meeting the requirements of subparagraph 3(o);...

Commercial or industrial development is the second biggest threat to open space. The assumption regarding the permitted exceptions to the prohibition here, which would not hold in all cases, is that they will not change the open space character of the land or cause any significant harm to the resources the easement is intended to protect. Note that forestry is included within the definition of "agricultural uses" in subparagraph 4(b) in **comment 17 (Reserved Rights: Express Restrictions)**.

CONSTRUCTION AND IMPROVEMENTS

(d) The placement, construction, or maintenance of any buildings, structures, or other improvements of any kind (including, without limitation, fences, roads, parking lots, and utility lines and related facilities) other than the following:

(1) The maintenance, renovation, expansion, or replacement of existing agricultural, residential, and related buildings, structures, and improvements in substantially their present location as shown on Exhibit ___; provided that any renovation, expansion, or replacement of an existing building, structure, or improvement may not substantially alter its character or function or increase its present height, or the land surface area it occupies, by more than [e.g., fifty (50)] per cent without the prior approval of Grantee;

---

12. The author is aware of one case (since resolved in the landowner's favor) where a deduction was challenged in the course of an IRS audit because the easement was silent on the question of transferable development rights.

(2) The placement or construction, after prior notice to Grantee, of additional buildings, structures, and improvements for agricultural purposes in the designated agricultural area described in Exhibit ___;

(3) The placement or construction, after prior notice to Grantee, of additional accessory structures and improvements for residential purposes (including, without limitation, private recreational facilities such as swimming pools and tennis courts but not including dwelling places of any kind) in the designated residential areas described in Exhibit ___;

(4) The placement or construction, after prior notice to Grantee, of not more than [e.g., three (3)] additional single-family residences in the designated residential areas described in Exhibit ___; provided that none of such additional residences may occupy more than _____ square feet of land surface area or exceed _____ feet in height without the prior approval of Grantee; and

(5) The placement or construction, after prior notice to Grantee, of facilities for the development and utilization of energy resources, including, without limitation, wind, solar, hydroelectric, methane, wood, alcohol, and fossil fuels, for use principally on the Property; provided that the design and location of any such facilities shall be subject to the prior approval of Grantee, and provided further that the development of fossil fuel resources shall be subject to the provisions of subparagraph 3(o);...

Generally, an easement is not intended to impinge on a grantor's existing activities or to limit their reasonable expansion—assuming they are not inconsistent with the purpose of the easement. The construction and improvements permitted by this subparagraph are treated as the physical extension of permitted uses. Since the landowner is in the best position to determine what buildings, structures, and other improvements are appropriate for permitted productive activities, like farming, or for enhancing the quality of domestic life, it is prudent to give him or her as much latitude as possible to make such decisions. Sample provisions (d)(l)-(5) attempt to do just that, on the assumption that the probability of adverse impacts from these limited activities is slight. Still, by highlighting certain concerns, such as size and location, and providing for prior notice and even approval under some circumstances, these provisions illustrate a full range of control. On real facts, tighter or looser controls than those in the sample might be desirable. In addition, of course, provision for still other facilities, such as guest cabins, worker housing, or specially designed wildlife-compatible fencing may be necessary under some circumstances, as may more specific restrictions on roads, utilities, or exterior lighting or on the conversion of a building's function or use—from agricultural to residential, say.[13] Coverage limitations on agricultural or

---

13. Regarding wildlife-compatible fencing, the Jackson Hole Land Trust has developed highly detailed standards for use under certain circumstances that might be adaptable to other areas.

accessory structures, similar to those in the sample relating to residences, are also sometimes imposed to avoid what might be considered excessive acreage being devoted to such factory farm structures as poultry sheds or hog parlors or to greenhouses.

Some parties will prefer to agree to many of the details of permitted future development, including the precise number, location, and design of all new buildings, before executing the easement. They should realize, however, that future landowners may find the original landowner's plans unsuitable to their needs. Under some circumstances, the right to develop the property further may be intentionally limited to the original grantors or their immediate successors, or a time limit may be imposed.

Some easements, particularly those with a dominant scenic element, include aesthetic considerations among the grantee's concerns and seek to limit a grantor's discretion in its choice of materials and designs for new construction. Typically, however, such matters are beyond the scope of an open space easement, and a grantee will seek to influence them, if at all, by subtler methods.[14]

Control of siting, based on agricultural and residential zones, is the principal device used by the sample to assure that the activities in question do not harm the conservation values of the hypothetical property. It should be noted that the failure to control the siting of any permitted development could result in real harm to conservation values and could leave the easement vulnerable to attack on grounds of vagueness.[15] It might also adversely affect qualification and valuation for tax purposes.

Site description by survey is preferred, although in some circumstances the use of maps, photographs, or natural boundaries may suffice. Alternative approaches include leaving site delineation to the future approval of the grantee, subject to specified limitations on size and location, or entirely excluding pre-approved sites from the area under easement.[16] The advantage to keeping such sites within the boundaries of the easement is that it preserves the grantee's right to ensure that any permitted development will be compatible with the easement. Most easements that include residential areas within their boundaries impose fewer restrictions on their use than on other areas under easement.

Subparagraph (d)(5) addresses a matter on which most easements are silent but that may have increasing importance in the future if, as many foresee, the sources of energy supply become more localized and diverse. In the usual case,

---

14. *See* Christine Carlson and Steven Durrant, *The Farm Landscape of Whatcom County: Managing Change Through Design* (Trust for Public Land 1985). This remarkable study of farm landscape aesthetics is indicative of the kind of education that is likely to be the most effective means of elevating a community's awareness of the impact of individual design choices on an area's scenic quality.

15. *See Parkinson v. Board of Assessors of Medford*, 398 Mass. 112, 495 N.E.2d 294 (1986).

16. For a discussion of some of the factors involved in dealing with future residential house sites, see Tom Howe, *Conservation Easements and Reserved House Lots,* LTA Exchange, Fall 1990, at 19.

there are not likely to be existing plans for improvements of this type, but since, among other things, they could help to maintain the viability of a farm or other land-based enterprise over the long haul, the landowner's freedom to employ them should be preserved. Windmills, small hydroelectric dams and turbines, biomass conversion systems, and solar devices are some of the energy production options that may prove useful in the future. Since improvements of this kind can have a direct impact on certain of the conservation resources an easement seeks to protect, prior approval of both location and design is recommended to assure compatibility. The number of such facilities might also be prescribed. But providing, as the sample does, that the energy produced be used "principally" on the property preserves some flexibility while imposing a limit that, in addition to whatever natural and practical limits there may be, ought to suffice in most cases.

The prohibition of the "placement" as well as construction of structures and "other improvements of any kind" is meant to be comprehensive, extending to trailers, towers, antennae, and the like. If any of these are of particular concern, express provision may, of course, be made for them.

Management Issues

The concerns addressed in subparagraphs (a), (c), and (d), dealing with subdivision, commercial development, and construction and improvements, are those most basic to open space preservation; they are found in one variant or another in all but the narrowest, most specialized easements. Subparagraph (b) addresses an emerging issue: what to do about development rights created by zoning or other forms of governmental regulation. What follows, typically, are provisions addressed to management issues, concerned in part with the protection of specific resources and in part with preserving the overall scenic quality of the land. Subparagraphs (e)-(o) are meant to give a sampling of the kinds of issues most frequently encountered; they are, however, neither comprehensive nor universal. In practice, the content of these provisions will vary markedly depending on the purpose of the easement, the region of the country involved, the use that the land will be put to, and most important, the particular features of the property in question.

SURFACE ALTERATION

> (e) Any alteration of the surface of the land, including, without limitation, the excavation or removal of soil, sand, gravel, rock, peat, or sod, except as may be required in the course of any activity expressly permitted herein or, after notice to the appropriate state agency and with the prior approval of Grantee, archaeological investigation; provided that construction materials, such as rock, dirt, sand, and gravel, may be taken for use in connection with permitted activities on the Property only from locations approved by Grantee;...

As this provision acknowledges, many of the activities permitted under the easement involve some disturbance of the land. In addition, it is a commonplace source of economy for farmers and other large landowners to use materials like sand and gravel that may be found on the property for their own construction projects. For most open space easements, such a limited use would not cause any problems. Where there is a scenic or other sensitive conservation element involved, however, site approval—as in the sample—is appropriate.

But a note of caution: it is possible to read the prohibition against surface mining in Section 170(h)(5)(B) of the Internal Revenue Code as extending to the surface removal of common construction materials, like sand and gravel, for private use. There is no support in the legislative history of this section for so broad an interpretation.[17] The clear focus of Congress was on large-scale commercial strip mining, which could destroy the conservation purpose of a gift, not the trivial impacts of a landowner's personal use of common surface materials. In fact, the regulations acknowledge that gravel pits may be among the existing man-made "incursions" on the property. *See* Treas. Reg. § 1.170A-14(g)(5)(i)(B). Nevertheless, some practitioners prefer to sidestep the issue by leaving the easement silent on it. Presumably, though, because this type of use is so commonplace, the parties would have to reach some understanding on the matter sooner or later. Because of the potential importance over the long term of the grantee's control over siting, the sample addresses it openly, up front.

The need for an exception for archaeological investigation will depend on circumstances, of course. If sites of archaeological interest are known or suspected to exist on the property, more detailed provision should be made for them.[18]

SOIL AND WATER

> (f) Any use or activity that causes or is likely to cause significant soil degradation or erosion or significant depletion or pollution of any surface or subsurface waters; provided that this prohibition shall not be construed as extending to agricultural operations and practices (including, without limitation, the use of agrichemicals such as fertilizers, pesticides, herbicides, and fungicides) that are substantially in accordance with a farm conservation plan prepared by the _____ County District Conservationist of the United States Department of Agriculture Natural Resource Conservation Service, or any successor or equivalent agency, which is reviewed and updated whenever a substantial change in operations is contemplated but, in any case, no less often than every ten (10) years;...

---

17. *See* U.S. Congress, House Committee on Ways and Means, *Miscellaneous Tax Bills: Charitable Deduction for Certain Contributions of Real Property for Conservation Purposes: Hearings on H.R. 4611 before the Subcommittee on Select Revenue Measures*, 96th Cong., 1st Sess. (1979), and *Minor Tax Bills: Deductions for Contributions of Certain Interests in Property for Conservation Purposes: Hearings on H.R. 7318 before the Subcommittee on Select Revenue Measures*, 96th Cong., 2nd Sess. (1980).

18. The Vermont Land Trust has developed a protocol and sample language for including the protection of archaeological values among the purposes of an open space easement.

Subparagraph (f) is intentionally broad. Because soil and water are the foundation upon which the long-range health of the land rests, it cuts across every permitted use of the property. A serious protection program for these resources, however, could involve considerable time and expense. It would be likely to entail the careful compilation and analysis of complex data on a regular basis to monitor the resources, as well as some kind of cooperative management mechanism for implementing any ameliorative measures that might be indicated. Few easement holders are in a position to take on that kind of responsibility, even where landowners are willing to cede it. Nevertheless, the grantee should have a hook for dealing with soil and water issues, if for no other reason than to enable it to prevent the gross harm to these resources that can result from relatively obvious causes (for example, gully erosion caused by the habitual use of off-road vehicles on severe slopes or stream pollution caused by uncontrolled stock access).

The proviso of this paragraph is intended to provide a means around the more difficult question of what to do about the cumulative effects that a landowner's primary productive use of the land—in this case farming—can have on these resources. Such effects, because they develop slowly over many years, may take some real expertise to detect. This is a long-term management matter and there are a number of ways to approach it. On some facts, a grantee may find the risk of sustained mismanagement so negligible that it will be comfortable accepting that risk and will impose no express requirements. On other facts, a grantee may choose to require an approved plan, or compel conformity with some recognized standards, or impose specific requirements based on its own criteria. A landowner's willing cooperation, though, will always be essential for any meaningful results. For this reason, and in keeping with the preference for minimal intrusiveness discussed at the outset, the sample illustrates a middle approach. No mandatory requirements are imposed, but a safe harbor is created for operations conducted under a conservation plan, giving the landowner a strong incentive to develop and maintain such a plan. If there are deficiencies in a plan, resulting in detriment to the resource, the grantee's recourse is to work with the landowner and the agency to make appropriate adjustments.

All will not agree that the Natural Resource Conservation Service is the highest authority in these matters; furthermore, its future ability to prepare individual farm plans may be constrained by budgetary limitations. Other sources of expertise, where available, may be substituted, of course. The point of the sample is only that in areas as complex as these, where knowledge and standards are evolving, the use of an objective performance standard, however imperfect, is likely to be the best approach both for the long-range management of the property and the long-range enforcement of the easement.

Where specific practices are known to be harmful, of course, their express prohibition may be in order. In some parts of the country, for example, municipal sewage sludge may be used for fertilizer even though it may contain heavy metals, and some easements prohibit the practice outright.

WETLANDS AND STREAM BUFFER

> (g) The draining, filling, dredging, or diking of the wetland areas described in Exhibit ____, including any enlargements thereof, or the cultivation or other disturbance of the soil within [e.g., fifty (50) feet] of the thread of _____ Creek, whose location is indicated on Exhibit ____;...

The location of any resource singled out for protection, like the creek and wetlands here, should be shown as accurately as possible on an accompanying map exhibit. Express agreement on the location of wetlands to be protected may be particularly important in light of the definitional strains that have developed in federal and state wetlands law in recent years. Any wetlands that may come into being in the future, other than as enlargements of existing wetlands, are not protected by this covenant, though, of course, the provision could be broadened to do so if desired. In places where beaver are active this could prove to be an especially sensitive issue. The cutting of trees or control of vegetation is not prohibited in the buffer area along the creek, although in some cases these additional restrictions might be appropriate. The appropriate size of the buffer will, of course, depend on particular circumstances.

PONDS, WATER COURSES, AND WELLS

> (h) The alteration or manipulation of the ponds, water courses, and wells located on the Property as shown on Exhibit ____, or the creation of new water impoundments, water courses, or wells, for any purpose other than permitted agricultural or residential uses of the Property or the limited energy development permitted under subparagraph 3(d)(5); provided that any new water impoundments, water courses, or wells for permitted agricultural or residential uses shall be located in the designated residential and agricultural areas described in Exhibit ____;...

Provisions that impinge on water rights can be extremely sensitive, particularly in the more arid regions of the West. In the western states, water rights constitute a valuable form of property that can be bought and sold separately from land, and familiarity with the water law of the jurisdiction is essential before venturing into this area. Water rights are controlled, quantified, and allocated in most western jurisdictions by a centralized regulatory authority, and landowners are likely to be circumspect about agreeing to any restrictions that would affect their allotment or any marketable entitlement they might have. On the other hand, a grantee will want to assure that water rights transfers have no adverse impact on the conservation values of the property and that critical rights are not permitted to lapse for failure to use them, as can occur in some states. The following, adapted from a provision developed by the Jackson Hole Land Trust, illustrates one way a balance might be struck:

> ...Grantors shall use their best efforts to assure the retention of any and all water rights appurtenant to the Property as are necessary to preserve and protect the conservation values of the Property and shall not transfer, encumber, sell, lease, or otherwise separate such rights from the Property or allow them to lapse due to nonuse or for any other reason;...

In the rest of the country, where the water supply is more abundant, the common law system of riparian rights governs the use of surface waters. Roughly stated, the right to use the water of a stream is incidental to and inseparable from the ownership of land adjoining the stream. It is a right held in common by all riparian landowners; downstream owners are entitled to the natural flow of a stream subject only to the reasonable diminution caused by upstream owners.

In the sample, how a landowner chooses to employ the water resources of the property for permitted uses is left to the landowner's discretion. This could be too broad a right on some facts. Some easements, for example, might require the grantee's approval of any new dam or impoundment or of its design and location, or might impose restrictions to protect fish or other water-related resources. (Note: sample subparagraph (d)(5) provides for grantee control over the design and location of energy development facilities. See "Construction and Improvements" above.) Other easements might prohibit any new water development altogether. The sample, however, assumes natural and practical limitations such that the landowner's exercise of rights under this provision would pose no significant threat to the conservation values of the property.

An issue not dealt with in the sample but becoming increasingly significant in some areas is the degree to which, short of amendment or condemnation, easement property can or should be used for the location of municipal water wells and related facilities. Under some circumstances, easement properties may be the only suitable or affordable potential sites for public water supply facilities. Although the issue can involve complex questions about the impacts of large scale withdrawals on water quality and quantity, as well as their interrelationship with agricultural uses, easement holders may wish to anticipate it with a prior approval clause.

TIMBER HARVESTING

(i) The pruning, cutting down, or other destruction or removal of trees located within the forest preserve areas described in Exhibit ___, except as necessary, in accordance with the current scientifically-based practices recommended by [e.g., the Natural Resource Conservation Service of the U.S. Department of Agriculture, or any successor or equivalent agency], to control or prevent hazard, disease, or fire or to maintain the designated open space areas described in Exhibit ___, or in accordance with subparagraph (j);

(j) The harvesting of trees within the forest preserve areas described in Exhibit ___ for any purpose other than the purposes set forth in subparagraph (i), except, after prior notice to Grantee, in accordance with a forest management plan, to be updated at least every [e.g., five (5)/ten (10)] years, that is prepared by a registered professional forester and [reviewed -or- approved] by Grantee and that is designed to assure the maintenance of good quality growing stock of [description of desired forest species/age classes mix], while protecting soil stability, water quality, and the other conservation values of the Property as identified in the Baseline Documentation, including, without limitation, scenic, riparian, and wildlife habitat values;...

These sample provisions are premised on a hypothetical working farm with substantial but subordinate forested acreage. The timber harvesting permitted by subparagraph (j) is not and is never likely to be the dominant use. The sample makes no attempt to limit the landowner's discretion to remove trees in farm and residential areas based on the judgment that no significant impact on the conservation values of the property would result from doing so. This, of course, would not be true for all properties. Depending on their purpose, some easements regulate these areas closely, even to the point of protecting individual trees, groves, or orchards. Similarly, no attempt is made here to regulate the landowner's right to control shrubs and other vegetation, though again, depending on the circumstances, such regulation might be appropriate.

The invocation of relevant standards, such as those promulgated by the Natural Resource Conservation Service, the U.S. Forest Service, state forestry agencies, or the Society of American Foresters, to guide the limited cutting and pruning permitted by subparagraph (i) should be bolstered by reference to specific written standards, where feasible.

A provision for maintaining designated open areas is frequently encountered. This can be particularly important in the Northeast where preventing forest encroachment on meadows or certain cultural resources, such as the foundation of an ancestral homesite, is a common concern. Other provisions are sometimes included for increasing arable acreage or preserving the view from a residence, or for obtaining firewood or lumber to be used on the property.

A requirement like that of subparagraph (j) for a professionally prepared forest management plan is considered essential by practitioners in this area where any significant timber harvesting is contemplated. The plan should provide an ecologically sound blueprint for reconciling the timber production and conservation goals for the property in question. It should contain a forest inventory and map and elaborate on the tree species mix, age classes, and products desired. It should also, of course, describe how the conservation values identified by the easement are to be protected, including any particularly sensitive values. Access, erosion control, and surface water protection are among the concerns that a plan must address, as are slash disposal, reseeding, reforestation, reclamation, and weed control. The grantee should have an opportunity to review the plan; prior approval might also be required, if desired.

Among terms sometimes encountered in this area, it should be noted that "sustained yield" forestry is concerned only with timber as opposed to other forest values, such as wildlife habitat, and does not necessarily preclude clear-cutting. Practitioners with any substantial involvement in forest land protection tend to avoid the phrase. "Selective cutting" methods, while they exclude clear-cutting (which might, in fact, be an appropriate, even preferred, method, under some circumstances) do not prevent high-grading (cutting only the best timber) or assure the maintenance of a variety of species or age classes among trees.[19]

---

19. The need for sustainable forest management is provoking some of the most innovative thinking currently going on in the conservation field generally and in easement practice in particular. *See* Mary Ellen Boelhower, *Forests Forever*, LTA Exchange, Spring 1995, at 4, and Laurie Wayburn, *Saving the Forests for the Trees, and Other Values*, The Back Forty, May-June 1994, at 1, for two good recent discussions dealing with easements.

COMMERCIAL FEEDLOTS

(k) The establishment or maintenance of any commercial feedlot, which is defined for the purposes of this Easement as a confined area or facility within which the land is not grazed or cropped at least annually and which is used to receive livestock that has been raised off the Property for feeding and fattening for market;...

This is a scenic protection provision, intended to prevent the property from becoming an unsightly stockyard. In many parts of the country this kind of use might be so infeasible as to require no specific mention. Elsewhere, the possible proliferation of greenhouses, poultry sheds, or hog parlors might be the issue. Setting limitations on acreage is one way to restrict these kinds of uses. Some easements seek to prohibit all husbandry practices, including certain types of poultry and dairy operations, that involve animals being kept in tightly confined environments. The judgment here, though, is that unless such uses pose a potential threat to the conservation values of the property, an easement is not the appropriate place to regulate them. It should be noted that the sample provision does not restrict the landowner's right to use permanent pens, corrals, and drylot feeding areas for animals raised on the property. The assumption, which may not be true in all cases, is that practical limitations would prevent such uses from having the degree of impact on the scenic quality of the property that a commercial feedlot could have.

WASTE DUMPS

(l) The processing, storage, dumping, or other disposal of wastes, refuse, and debris on the Property, except for nonhazardous and nontoxic materials generated by activities permitted herein; provided that only the site indicated in Exhibit ___ may be used for this purpose, or such other site or sites as Grantee may approve;...

Almost every easement has a provision dealing with dumps. When a property is especially sensitive, an absolute prohibition might be in order. Most large properties, however, have some capacity for on-site waste disposal, and the important thing is to assure that the scenic and other conservation values of the property are protected by finding an inconspicuous and otherwise appropriate place for it. Although the sample does not do so, some easements distinguish between vegetative and other forms of waste. As for hazardous and toxic wastes, these are covered by paragraphs 8.3-8.6 of the model discussed at **comment 26 (Representations, Warranties, and Remediation)**.

STORAGE TANKS AND UTILITY SYSTEMS

(m) The installation of underground storage tanks or the above-ground installation of new utility systems or extensions of existing utility systems, including, without limitation, water, sewer, power, fuel, and communication lines and related facilities, but excluding systems for irrigating the Property;...

The prohibition of underground storage tanks reflects the fact that fuel storage tank leakage has been recognized as a major source of soil and water pollution in recent years. As for the requirement for placing new utilities underground, this may be more or less important depending on the degree of aesthetic refinement considered appropriate in the region of the country where the property is located. Placing utility lines underground can be substantially more expensive than above-ground installation. Under certain circumstances, it may even be more disruptive, or even destructive, of conservation values. Whether or not undergrounding is to be required, a grantee might want to add the authority to review or approve new utility installations or the upgrade or relocation of existing lines and facilities.

SIGNS AND BILLBOARDS

(n) The placement of any signs or billboards on the Property, except that signs whose placement, number, and design do not significantly diminish the scenic character of the Property may be displayed to state the name and address of the Property and the names of persons living on the Property, to advertise or regulate on-site activities permitted pursuant to paragraph 4, to advertise the Property for sale or rent, and to post the Property to control unauthorized entry or use; and...

A provision of this type may serve to supplement or reinforce existing governmental regulations in some locations. Some easements go well beyond the sample and specify the location, size, and number of permitted signs and prohibit their artificial illumination. Having prohibited billboards outright, the sample makes the assumption, which may not be justified in all cases, that any problems that might arise over permitted signs are manageable within the stated "scenic character" constraint.

MINERAL DEVELOPMENT

(o) The exploration for, or development and extraction of, minerals and hydrocarbons by any surface mining method or any other method that would significantly impair or interfere with the conservation values of the Property. Prior to engaging in any mineral exploration, development, or extraction by any method not otherwise prohibited by this paragraph, Grantors must notify Grantee and submit a plan for Grantee's approval that provides for minimizing the adverse effects of the operation on the conservation values of the Property. In addition to such other measures as may be required to protect the conservation values of the Property, the plan must provide for: (1) preserving the quantity and quality of all surface and ground water; (2) concealing all facilities or otherwise locating them so as to be compatible with existing topography and landscape to the greatest practicable extent; and (3) restoring any altered physical features of the land to their original state.

This provision addresses the requirements of Section 170(h)(5) of the Internal Revenue Code and Sections 1.170A-14(g)(4) and (5)(ii) of the IRS regulations, which prohibit surface mining and any other method of mining that is inconsistent with the particular purposes of an easement. The regulations contemplate that permitted mining may have "limited, localized impact" on the property so long as it is not "irremediably destructive of significant conservation interests." Designing production facilities to be compatible with existing topography and landscape and requiring reclamation to the "original state" of the land are given as examples of ways to meet this test. In addition, prior notice to the grantee is required. The sample exceeds this requirement by requiring prior approval of a mitigation plan.

There are certain long-range effects of mining, including subsidence, that may need to be considered depending on the circumstances. In addition, it should be noted that even under the best of circumstances the immediate surface impact of subsurface mining, whether for oil and gas or other minerals, can be substantial—involving, for example, roads, drill holes, well heads, pipelines, pump stations, and other temporary structures and the generation of mine tailings and other wastes. For these reasons many grantees seek, where possible, to prohibit mining entirely or to limit it to off-site access.

In the few areas of the country where geothermal resources occur, express provision should be made for them in this paragraph.

16. Reserved Rights (paragraph 4)

This provision is a restatement of what is likely to be the law in most jurisdictions anyway. An easement is a conveyance of a partial interest in property; rights not conveyed are reserved. Here, as throughout the model, consistency with the purpose of the easement is expressly made the ultimate test of the landowner's rights. This is a useful expression of the parties' intent. Even without an express statement of the consistency standard, however, a court would be likely to apply it in a dispute over the scope of the grantor's reserved rights. It is a general rule of conveyancing law that a reservation inconsistent with the estate conveyed is void as repugnant to the grant. Like most common law principles, though, the repugnancy doctrine is susceptible to manipulation, and courts, in trying to carry out the intent of the instrument, seek whenever they can to reconcile reservations with the grant to give effect to both. The content of the express restrictions and reservations, along with the description of the conservation values of the property in the recitals and, if applicable, the baseline data, are collectively the best available source of guidance for applying the consistency standard to activities that have not been expressly provided for as well as those that have. They should be drafted with this secondary function in mind.

Paragraph 15.7 of the model provides that the terms of the easement apply to the grantors' successors as well as the grantors. Nevertheless, to foreclose any possibility of the reservations being construed as merely personal to the grantors, explicit reference is made to the grantors' successors here. In addition, to avoid any confusion regarding an important matter, the landowner's right to control access by third parties is made clear.

It should be noted that in certain western states, where water rights are a sensitive issue, landowners may insist on an express reservation of water rights. In the form most frequently encountered, water rights are described as:

> All right, title, and interest in and to all tributary and nontributary water, water rights, and related interests in, on, under, or appurtenant to the Property.

As discussed in **comment 15 (Prohibited Uses: Express Restrictions)** under "Development Rights," where residual transferable development rights are intended to be conveyed along with the easement, development rights that might be needed to undertake any permitted construction on the property should be expressly reserved.

17. Reserved Rights: Express Reservations (paragraph 4)

Since consistency with the purpose of the easement is the ultimate test of the permissibility of any activity, most grantors understandably want to make it clear that the uses they intend to pursue are not inconsistent with the easement they are granting. The express reservations function as a stipulation to that effect. As a formal matter, most express reservations could be drafted as qualifications of or exceptions to the express restrictions of the preceding section. In some easements that is how they appear, with the reserved rights provision then requiring no more than a brief general statement similar to the introductory portion of paragraph 4 of the model. Some permitted uses like mining or building are so heavily regulated that their logical place is among the restrictions. Many find it useful, however, for convenience of reference, to isolate the most fundamental of the landowner's reserved rights from the restrictions, and the sample that follows is an example of that approach. The reservations cannot be fully understood in isolation, however, any more than the restrictions can. The two sections are interconnected and must be read together.

Sample Reservations

In keeping with the policy preference for minimizing the intrusiveness of the easement (discussed in **comment 15 (Prohibited Uses: Express Restrictions)**) the scope of the grantor's reserved rights should be as broad as the conservation purpose of the easement will permit. In the context of a typical open space easement, the ability of the grantor to make economically viable, productive uses of the property may be as important to the long-term preservation of the open space character of the land as the easement itself. The following paragraphs have been drafted with that consideration in mind. Again, as always, it should be understood that this represents only one mix out of an unlimited range of possibilities, and that the rights enumerated here remain subject to the express terms of paragraph 3 (prohibited uses).

(a) To reside on the Property;

(b) To engage in any and all agricultural uses of the Property. For the purposes of this Easement "agricultural uses" shall be defined as: breeding, raising, boarding, pasturing, and grazing livestock of every nature and description; breeding and raising bees, fish, poultry, and other fowl; planting, raising, harvesting, and producing agricultural, aquacultural, horticultural, and forestry crops and products of every nature and description; and the primary processing, storage, and sale, including direct retail sale to the public, of crops and products harvested and produced principally on the Property;

(c) To engage in any business that is conducted by, and in the home of, a person residing on the Property or that involves the provision of goods or services incidental to, and occupies structures used principally for, the agricultural uses of the Property; and

(d) To engage in and permit others to engage in recreational uses of the Property, including, without limitation, hunting and fishing, that require no surface alteration or other development of the land.

The sample assumes that the primary productive use of the hypothetical property for the foreseeable future will be agriculture and that agriculture is itself an open space value worthy of protection. (In some easements preserving farming is the central purpose.) The intent is to authorize the continuation and reasonable expansion of existing agricultural operations with negligible interference from the grantee. In addition—in order to give the landowners as much flexibility as possible to adapt to changing market conditions over the years—the subparagraph (b) definition of "agricultural uses" goes beyond conventional farming activities to embrace a broad range of productive open space uses, including, expressly or by implication, fish hatching, greenhouse cultivation, tree farming, sod farming, hydroponics, and timber production. Under a given set of circumstances one or more of these uses might be inappropriate and, if so, should be specifically restricted or prohibited.

Both parties should realize, however, that existing activities are not likely to exhaust the possibilities of compatible uses and should make an effort to provide some sense of the scope of the permissible. Defining terms—even those that, like "agricultural uses," may at first blush seem self-explanatory—is likely to be the best way to do this. It will also go a long way toward preventing unnecessary misunderstandings between the original parties or their successors later on.

Recognizing the economic importance of related secondary activities to many farm operations, the sample permits the processing and retail sale of products produced principally on the property. In addition, the sample permits home occupations and secondary agricultural trades, which might include, for example, farm mechanics, blacksmithing, or riding instruction. There could be reason in some cases to impose tighter restrictions on secondary activities than the sample does or to deal with them in greater detail. There may be particular concern, for example, over the number and design of structures used in the direct sale of agricultural products. Under most conditions, however, the outright prohibition of these activities is not likely to be necessary to protect the open space values of a property.

Some easements contain provisions for fish and wildlife protection. The sample restrictions show concern for habitat protection but do not get involved in wildlife management. In some areas of the country and under some circumstances restrictions on fishing and hunting may be called for, but they can be difficult to monitor and enforce. The sample assumes a factual situation under which reliance on state regulation in this area is sufficient. The sample also assumes that using the hypothetical property for low-impact open space recreation, even on a commercial basis, would be no less compatible with the conservation values of the property than current agricultural uses.

18. Notice of Intention to Undertake Certain Permitted Actions and Grantee Approval (paragraphs 5.1 and 5.2)

The IRS requires that the grantor agree to notify the grantee in writing prior to exercising reserved rights that might have an adverse impact on the conservation values the easement is intended to protect. *See* Treas. Reg. § 1.170A-14(g)(5)(ii). It is incumbent on the parties to determine which permitted activities reach that threshold and tie them into the notice provision. (See sample provisions (d)(2)-(5), (j), and (o) in **comment 15 (Prohibited Uses: Express Restrictions)**.) Some drafters add a catch-all clause as well, such as the following introductory language:

> Grantors agree to notify Grantee prior to undertaking any activity that may have a material adverse impact on the conservation values of the Property, and specifically prior to undertaking certain permitted activities, as provided in paragraphs _____. The purpose of this notice requirement is to afford Grantee...etc.

The IRS requires only that the grantor *notify* the grantee prior to exercising potentially harmful reserved rights; the grantee's *prior approval* is not required. Nevertheless the grantee may want to negotiate for approval authority where it considers the activity in question to be sufficiently sensitive to warrant it. (See sample provisions (d)(1), (d)(4)-(5), (e), (j), (l), and (o) in **comment 15 (Prohibited Uses: Express Restrictions)**.)

Often, a "reasonable" basis for withholding an approval is expressly required. A reasonableness requirement implies that approval authority will be exercised in good faith, in a fair, nondiscriminatory manner. A denial cannot be arbitrary or capricious; there must be a reason for it that is rationally related to the purpose of the easement and the protection of the conservation values of the Property. Personal taste, convenience, or sensibility are not enough. In some cases, however, particularly where sensitive natural habitats or ecosystems are involved, or where an added margin of protection is otherwise desired, a grantee might seek to be vested with absolute discretion to permit or prohibit a proposed activity, in an attempt to foreclose the possibility of being second-guessed. The second sentence of paragraph 5.2 might then read:

> The granting or withholding of approval shall be in Grantee's sole discretion.

Whether, however, one can, in fact, do more than shift the burden to the Grantor to show that approval authority has been exercised in an unreasonable manner will depend on the law of the jurisdiction in question. The trend, represented in a growing minority of states, is to recognize an implied covenant of good faith and fair dealing in every contract, which is then interpreted to be the equivalent of a reasonableness requirement.[20]

Consistency with the purpose of the easement is the fundamental determining factor for granting or withholding approval. More specific criteria can be stated if desired, and the right to issue conditional approvals might also be expressed. If the grantee does not have approval authority and a dispute arises concerning the consistency of a proposed activity, the grantee's only recourse is to pursue its judicial or other dispute resolution remedies under the easement. If the grantee does have approval authority, and the grantor is to remain in compliance with the terms of the easement, it becomes the grantor's burden to seek resolution of a dispute.

The exercise of review and approval rights can represent a substantial administrative burden in some cases. Care should be taken to allow sufficient time for careful study of a proposal. More specific documentation might be expressly required, as appropriate, including copies of plans, drawings, zoning or planning board applications and approvals, permits, exemptions, waivers, and the like. Provision might also be made for reimbursement of the costs incurred in undertaking a review.

Approvals and denials should be given in writing as the model provision requires. Particular care should be taken to document the reasons for a denial, grounding the explanation in the express terms of the easement itself. If a grantee's action is subsequently challenged, the contemporaneous written explanation for it will provide an important evidentiary record.

To assure grantors that approval decisions will be made in a timely fashion, some easements provide that a grantee's failure to respond in the stated time period shall be deemed an approval, so long as the activity in question is not contrary to any express restriction in the easement. Of course, under most circumstances, a grantor is likely to consider an extension of the time for review preferable to a timely denial.

19. Grantee's Remedies (paragraphs 6.1-6.5)

Section 6 ensures that the grantee will have the full panoply of enforcement powers for protecting not only the conservation values of the property but all its rights under the easement. The IRS requires that an easement provide a right of enforcement "by appropriate legal proceedings," including the right to require restoration. *See* Treas. Reg. § 1.170A-14(g)(5)(ii).

---

20. *See Kendall v. Ernest Pestana, Inc.*, 40 Cal. 3d 488, 220 Cal. Rptr. 818, 709 P.2d 837 (1985), for just such an interpretation with regard to a consent provision in a lease, and for an extended discussion of the issue generally.

Paragraph 6.1. Provision for notice and an opportunity to cure violations is customary, but the grantee should be given the right to look to its remedies without notice when necessary, in its judgment, to prevent or limit damage to the conservation values of the property **(Paragraph 6.4)**. Some easements provide for recordation of the notice of violation. The model avoids this approach because of the danger that, were the landowner to prevail against the allegations referred to in the grantee's notice, the landowner might be able to sue the grantee for slander of title. In addition, such notices unnecessarily clog the record. Recordation of the easement puts the world on notice of the possibility that a violation may exist, obligating interested parties to satisfy themselves of the landowner's compliance by obtaining estoppel certificates (paragraph 12 of the model easement) or otherwise. Consequently, a recorded notice of violation is superfluous. On the other hand, once suit is filed, recording a notice of *lis pendens* (literally, "suit pending") is appropriate, and unless the case is frivolous, the filing is protected as a necessary adjunct of the court's exercise of jurisdiction.

Paragraph 6.2. This paragraph is inescapably technical. The following is a brief explanation of the terms that might be puzzling to a lay reader. The distinction between "an action at law or in equity" is deeply rooted in the history of the common law. In general, an action at law is for damages; a suit in equity is for injunctive relief. In modern practice, these actions are combined and heard by the same judge who is empowered to grant both kinds of relief. Regarding injunctions, an order *"ex parte"* is one issued on the behalf of one party without notice to the other, usually under emergency circumstances, which is often the case with temporary restraining orders. A temporary restraining order is issued for only a very limited period of time, and determination of the merits is expedited. After a hearing, a preliminary injunction may be issued to preserve the status quo pending trial. Final judgment may result in a permanent injunction. Injunctions can require a person to refrain from or, more rarely, to perform some act, termed "prohibitive" and "mandatory" injunctions respectively.

One remedy not provided here that is sometimes seen in conservation easements is self-help: the right of a grantee to peaceably enter the property to abate a violation and charge any costs incurred to the landowner. There are circumstances where the availability of this remedy is appropriate, especially if the grantee has substantial management responsibilities. In a typical open space easement, however, where the landowner maintains an active, continuous presence on the property, an attempt to exercise the self-help remedy could easily create more problems than it prevents. Landowners are likely to view self-help as too invasive, and even if a grantee is selective in its use, self-help could engender hostility. In addition, exercise of a self-help remedy could result in increasing the grantee's exposure to liability for physical conditions on the property, including toxic conditions (see discussion at **comment 26 (Representations, Warranties, and Remediation)**), and for payment of contractors.

Paragraph 6.3. With respect to damages, where appropriate, consideration might be given to adding a provision entitling the grantee to recover the value of any minerals, crops, timber, or other materials or resources removed from the property in violation of the easement. As for the reference to loss of "scenic, aesthetic or environmental values," conservation easements may break new ground in this area, particularly if support can be found in the state enabling statutes for such "creative" relief. The terms, as used here, track one such statute.

Paragraph 6.5. In this paragraph, the model attempts to remove some of the legal obstacles to obtaining an injunction or "specific performance" of the easement agreement by having the grantors agree up-front that damages are an inadequate remedy for violations of the easement. The grantee's remedies are described as cumulative and nonexclusive in order to give the grantee the widest latitude to enforce the easement. One available remedy not expressly enumerated is the right to appeal to a court to interpret the easement and issue a "declaratory judgment" regarding its terms even if no other relief is required.

20. Costs of Enforcement (paragraph 6.6)

Many easements require the grantor to bear the grantee's enforcement costs. Drafters should exercise caution in this area, however. In some jurisdictions, contractual provisions for payment by one party of the other's court costs, including attorneys' fees, are made reciprocal by statute. In these jurisdictions, the prevailing party is entitled to payment of its costs and fees by the other party regardless of what the contract provides.

While reciprocity does have the beneficial effect of forcing both parties to be equally circumspect with regard to pursuing litigation, there is concern among some practitioners that its effect on enforcement, particularly for small land trusts, would be too chilling. In addition, some land trusts regard a grantor's unilateral undertaking to pay the costs of enforcement as a way of reducing the amount of endowment they might otherwise need to seek from original donors, who might view the clause as affecting future owners more than themselves in any case.

Some grantors may insist on reciprocity, however. If so, the last clause of paragraph 6.6 might be modified as follows:

> ...provided, however, that if Grantors ultimately prevail in a judicial enforcement action brought by Grantee, Grantee shall bear both its own costs and Grantors' reasonable costs and expenses of suit, including, without limitation, reasonable attorneys' fees.

Some drafters limit the grantee's liability to costs of suit, which are assessed by the court, and exclude attorneys' fees. Public agencies, in particular, may be restricted by law in their ability to enter into contractual agreements to pay another party's litigation costs or attorneys' fees.

"Ultimately prevail" might be defined as "a final decision in favor of Grantor by the highest court having jurisdiction and ruling on the matter." Depending on the jurisdiction, a trial court may have wide discretion to determine who is the prevailing party where there is any doubt.

Note that the range of costs involved is not the same for both parties. By their nature, certain costs, like the costs of restoration, will always be the obligation of the grantor.

Statutes dealing specifically with conservation easements may make independent provision for costs and fees.

21. Forbearance and Waiver of Certain Defenses (paragraphs 6.7-6.8)

Paragraphs 6.7 and 6.8 of the model easement attempt to remove technical defenses to enforcement of the easement. The extent to which these clauses are enforceable may vary from state to state.

It should be noted that, in most jurisdictions, a grantee's exercise of discretion in enforcement matters is subject to governmental oversight. If a grantee is seriously derelict, the attorney general of the state in which the easement is located may have standing, under the state's general supervisory authority over charitable institutions, to ensure that the easement is enforced. In addition, third parties may be given enforcement rights—in some cases by statute, in others by the terms of the easement itself.

The defense of "laches" is based on undue delay. "Estoppel" is based on the prior statement or act of one party in reliance on which another party does something he or she would not otherwise have done. "Prescription" is the equivalent in the easement context of "adverse possession."

Waivers are not favored by the courts, who tend to scrutinize them closely. Some drafters, in recognition of this fact, seek to bolster the language of paragraph 6.8 to reflect relevant case law. Additional language might include a representation by grantors acknowledging that they have carefully reviewed the easement, that they have been advised by counsel as to the meaning of its various terms and requirements, and that the waiver in question is made in light of, and with full knowledge of, its provisions. Another approach is to explain why the waiver is justified, citing, for example, Grantee's limited presence on the property and limited resources for monitoring compliance.

22. Acts Beyond Grantor's Control (paragraph 6.9)

This paragraph is an important common sense limitation on a landowner's liability. Not only "acts of God," but a landowner's emergency measures in response to such acts, are beyond the scope of the easement. Some easements go beyond the natural causes listed here to deal with the actions of third parties, though there is disagreement about how far to go in this direction. The purpose of an exculpatory clause of this type is, as a matter of fairness, to free landowners of responsibility for damage to the property they are powerless to prevent. It is not meant to shift the responsibility for overseeing third party activities to the grantee. Tenant farmers, contract loggers, construction workers—anyone whose presence on the land has been authorized by the grantor—should remain the grantor's responsibility, however "unauthorized" one or another of their actions might prove to be. Even trespassers whose injurious actions a grantor might have anticipated or prevented ought to remain the grantor's responsibility, since the grantor is likely to be in a better position to undertake whatever defensive measures are necessary. Consequently, if provision for the acts of third parties is to be made, the following limited language is suggested:

> ...fire, flood, storm, earth movement, *and acts of trespassers that Grantors could not reasonably have anticipated or prevented*...etc.

Provision might also be made for enforcement against trespassers, as in the following:

> In the event the terms of this Easement are violated by acts of trespassers that Grantors could not reasonably have anticipated or prevented, Grantors agree, at Grantee's option, to join in any suit, to assign their right of action to Grantee, or to appoint Grantee their attorney-in-fact, for the purposes of pursuing enforcement action against the responsible parties.[21]

23. Access (paragraph 7)

This paragraph negates any implication of third party access rights. Where visual access is a component of an easement, some drafters insert the word "physical" modifying "access" to distinguish between the two types. Limitations on public access do not affect the deductibility of conservation easements, unless the conservation purpose of the easement would be undermined without public access. *See* Treas. Reg. § § 1.170A-14(d)(2)(ii), (d)(3)(iii), (d)(4)(ii)(C), and (d)(5)(iv). Thus, for example, recreational or educational easements require "substantial and regular" public access, and scenic easements require substantial "visual" access, as do easements with an historical component. But otherwise—in the absence of any state law to the contrary—the kind and degree of public access to be conveyed, if any, is purely a matter for the parties to decide.

Where public access is contemplated, provision is usually made for it in the "Purpose" or "Rights of Grantee" sections of the easement, and depending on the type of easement involved, terms governing the time, place, and manner of its exercise will be spelled out in greater or lesser detail, or left to the discretion of the grantee. Alternatively, particularly in an educational easement, where some third party, such as a research university, might be a principal beneficiary of access privileges, a separate memorandum of understanding governing the terms of access might be referenced. Where the preservation of intended visual, as opposed to physical, access requires some degree of maintenance or forbearance—as, for example, by limiting the height or density of trees or restricting the use of fencing or other barriers or obstructions—express provision must be made for this as well.

---

21. For an interesting case study involving an easement violation by a trespasser, see Sarah Thorne, *Dealing with Violations: Lessons from a Case Study*, LTA Exchange, Spring 1989, at 1.

The fact that no public access is conveyed by the easement does not preclude the landowner from permitting such access (see paragraph 4 of the model easement, regarding reserved rights) unless the easement expressly restricts the right to do so—as it might, for instance, in a natural ecosystem easement. In addition, the easement does not affect any pre-existing access rights that may have been created over the years, whether expressly or by prescription, by implied dedication, or by operation of the public trust doctrine.

It is worth noting that in order to increase opportunities for public access to both public and private lands many states have passed so-called recreational use statutes, which are designed to insulate landowners from liability for injury to persons or property that may occur as a result of their opening their lands to the public. The degree of protection these statutes afford can vary substantially, however, and practitioners are advised to review both the statutes themselves and the case law interpreting them carefully before relying on them.[22]

24. Costs, Legal Requirements, and Liabilities (paragraph 8.1)

Sections 1 through 7 of the model easement constitute the real substance of the easement; sections 8 through 15 consist of necessary but ancillary technical provisions—the fine print.

The landowner should continue to bear all the normal costs of land ownership unless the grantee is given an active role in managing the property. The grantee typically bears the cost of monitoring compliance with the easement and keeping the baseline data current, although increasingly grantees are requesting that grantors make a one-time grant of funds for these purposes. Some maintenance obligations, such as, for example, mowing of grasses and cutting or thinning of trees and shrubs to comply with governmental fire management regulations, may arise or persist, directly or indirectly, because of the existence of an easement. If they are to remain the landowner's responsibility, express reference to them might be made here.

Practice varies on whether to impose an affirmative obligation to maintain liability insurance coverage. Many easements are silent on the issue; some go beyond requiring coverage and obligate the landowner to include the grantee as an "additional insured." Of course, protection under an individual landowner's policy does not obviate the need for commercial general liability coverage as part of a grantee organization's comprehensive risk management program. Where a right of public access is granted by an easement, the roles may be reversed, and

---

22. *See* Goldstein *et. al.*, *Recreational Use Statutes: Why They Don't Work*, LTA Exchange, Spring 1990, at 10; Gail Secor, *Recreational Use Statutes: Making Them More Effective*, The Back Forty, December 1990-January 1991, at 9; see also Chris Cole, *Tort Liability and Land Trusts: How Safe Are You?*, The Back Forty, November 1990, at 1, 4-5. For a recent case liberally construing a recreational use statute in favor of a governmental landowner, see *Sandler v. Commonwealth*, 419 Mass. 334, 644 N.E.2d 641 (1995).

a landowner may seek to be named an additional insured under a grantee organization's liability policy.[23]

Under some circumstances, casualty loss coverage could become an issue as well. In the historic preservation context, where the potential for suffering a casualty loss that could defeat the purpose of an easement is a central concern, detailed clauses dealing with casualty damage, restoration, and insurance are routine. Among other things, preservation easements may give the grantee the right to review and approve the amount and type of coverage and to be notified in advance of any changes in coverage. Some even go so far as to empower the grantee to purchase the insurance directly, backed by a lien for reimbursement, if the grantor fails to do so. In the typical conservation easement, however, absent an historic or archaeological feature whose destruction would be fatal to the easement's underlying purpose, provisions of this kind are rare.

Reference is made to legal requirements, such as the need to obtain applicable building permits and the like, to make it clear that conveyance of an easement does not obviate compliance with governmental requirements for construction and land use. Misunderstandings can sometimes arise in this area, particularly where an easement involves a governmental grantee or some other form of governmental participation.

The law regarding contractors' liens, known as mechanic's or materialman's liens, varies from jurisdiction to jurisdiction. In some states it is clear that the grantee's interest would not be affected by them. In others the language of the relevant statutes is broad enough to reach an easement, but theoretical problems having to do with the nature of conservation easements and the limitations on the kinds of entities entitled to hold them cast doubt on whether liens of this kind could ever attach to them. The model provides for them here as a matter of prudence. Drafters should consult local law to determine what steps, if any, need to be taken to protect against such liens.

25. Taxes (paragraph 8.2)

The special attention given to property taxes here is prompted by the fact that a grant of an easement could give rise in some jurisdictions to a shift or increase in tax liability.

All other things being equal, the creation of an easement whose restrictions lower the market value of a property should lead to a reduction in property taxes but, absent special legislation, this effect is not automatic. In some jurisdictions, the transfer of an easement might trigger a reassessment of the property, which if long overdue could lead to an increase. In addition, depending on local law, a conservation easement might be considered a separately taxable interest. Although the law in this area has been evolving for the better, most grantees still seek to insulate themselves from any tax liability in terms similar to the model.

---

23. See discussion in Douglas Muir, *Public Access and Landowner Liability*, LTA Exchange, Spring 1994, at 10, 12.

Where state law does require property tax assessors to take a conservation easement's effect on market value into account, reference to the appropriate statutes might also be made.

Special precaution is required in the minority of jurisdictions where tax liens are senior to all other interests in the property. There, a grantee will want to have the authority to pay delinquent taxes in order to protect its interest in the property against foreclosure in a tax sale. The following language is representative:

> ...Grantee is authorized, but in no event obligated, to make or advance any payment of taxes, upon [e.g., three (3)] days prior written notice to Grantors, in accordance with any bill, statement, or estimate procured from the appropriate authority, without inquiry into the validity of the taxes or the accuracy of the bill, statement, or estimate, and the obligation created by such payment shall bear interest until paid by Grantors at the lesser of ___ percentage points over the prime rate of interest from time to time charged by [designated bank] or the maximum rate allowed by law.

Wherever, as here, provision is made for interest payments, the drafter should take care to stay within the limits imposed by any state usury laws.

For additional protection, some easements authorize the grantee to impose a lien of its own to recover any costs the grantee may incur in this context or, in some cases, to secure all of the grantee's costs or advances relating to the easement, regardless of the context. (Although these contractual lien provisions are encountered most often in the historical easement context, where self-help provisions are sometimes employed, they have found their way into some open space easements as well.) It is an approach one associates with commercial transactions, and potential grantors may find it objectionable. Still, a contractual lien is undeniably the most efficient way to secure the grantee's position when the grantee is forced to expend funds to protect its rights under the easement, so its attraction is hard to resist, particularly if the easement includes significant self-help provisions. Where this approach is used, care must be taken to comply with local law governing the creation of a lien, as well as to structure the remedy in a way that will not interfere with the landowner's ability to use the property to secure future financing. It should be noted that, even without a contractual lien, in the rare instance where a grantee elects to make a defensive expenditure it can, if necessary, sue for repayment and, if successful, record a judgment lien.

26. Representations, Warranties, Remediation, and Control (paragraphs 8.3-8.5)

No legal development in recent years has created more concern among land conservation organizations than the broad expansion of liability for toxic and hazardous wastes that has occurred as a result of the federal Comprehensive Environmental Response, Compensation, and Liability Act of 1980 (CERCLA) and corresponding state statutes. The sweep of this remedial legislation—which holds anyone in the chain of title to a contaminated site potentially responsible for its cleanup, regardless of fault—is breathtaking. Defenses are limited: an innocent purchaser, who did not know and had no reason to know of a release of hazardous substance, can escape liability only if "all appropriate inquiry" into prior ownership and use of the property was made at the time of purchase. Due diligence in satisfying this requirement will vary from case to case but is likely to require, at minimum, a physical inspection of the property and surrounding properties and an investigation into their land use history through interviews and a documentary review. If a potential problem surfaces, more extensive—and expensive—professional environmental assessments will be required. CERCLA defenses, limited as they are, do not apply in non-CERCLA suits brought by adjoining landowners or as a threshold bar to an EPA cleanup order.

Recent federal case law, if followed, indicates that easement holders will not be considered "owners" for purposes of CERCLA liability.[24] An easement holder with substantial day-to-day involvement in management of a property or with significant affirmative rights could still be found liable as an "operator," however.[25] Whether a holder's less active stewardship obligations rise to this level is an open question. It is clear, however, that an easement holder that becomes involved in the cleanup of hazardous materials could incur liability as a disposal "arranger" under the law. [26]

The necessity of performing a due diligence investigation prior to the acquisition of an interest in real property, whether in fee or less than fee—or, as in an appurtenant easement transaction, both—is an accepted fact of life for land conservation organizations these days. Depending on the circumstances—and grantees will have to determine on a case-by-case basis what is necessary and what is overkill—contractual protections may also be sought, in terms similar to or more or less comprehensive than those set forth in the model.[27] Knowledgeable legal counsel is critical in this area, which is fraught with traps. Of course, the level of financial protection these provisions afford depends on the strength of the resources a grantor has to back them up. They serve a potentially important evidentiary function as well, however, by clarifying the parties' intent regarding responsibility for these matters, and particularly for any cleanup. As paragraph 8.5 is intended to make clear, management and control remain squarely with the landowner.

---

24. *See Long Beach Unified School District v. Dorothy B. Godwin California Living Trust*, 32 F.3d 1364 (9th Cir. 1994); *Grand Trunk Western Railroad Company v. Acme Belt Recoating, Inc.*, 859 F.Supp. 1125 (W.D. Mich 1994). The court in *Long Beach* specifically mentioned "'scenic' easements" in support of its argument that holding easement holders liable would "disserve the statute's purposes...and vastly and unjustifiably increase the potential number of CERCLA defendants."

25. *See Pennsylvania v. Union Gas Company*, 491 U.S. 1, 109 S.Ct. 1960 (1989).

26. *See* Comprehensive Environmental Response, Compensation, and Liability Act (CERCLA), 42 U.S.C. § 9607(a)(3).

27. Contractual allocations of responsibility, assuming they are valid under state law, have been upheld by the federal courts. *See* Jacqueline Warren, *Indemnification: A Defense Against CERCLA Financial Responsibility*, LTA Exchange, Winter 1994, at 16, and cases there cited. However, as noted in a footnote to the Preface on page x, proposed legislation under consideration in Congress could obviate any need for contractual protections in most easements.

Paragraph 8.3, as well as the corresponding indemnity clause of paragraph 8.6, is drafted broadly. It covers environmental laws, including federal and state hazardous waste laws, as well as any other laws that might affect a property or its use. Subparagraph 8.3(a) may be too broad in circumstances where a property has seen extensive farming or other use where hazardous materials are likely to have been employed, however responsibly. An alternative in such cases might read:

(a) Any handling, transportation, storage, treatment or use of any substance defined, listed, or otherwise classified pursuant to any federal, state, or local law, regulation, or requirement as hazardous, toxic, polluting, or otherwise contaminating to the air, water, or soil, or in any way harmful or threatening to human health or the environment, that has occurred on the Property prior to the date of this Easement has been in compliance with all applicable federal, state, and local laws, regulations, and requirements. No deposit, disposal, or other release of any hazardous substance or toxic waste has occurred on or from the Property, which is free of all such contamination;...

The objective of paragraph 8.3, of course, is to avoid surprises. Although the grantors' representations are made "to the best of their knowledge," grantors are required to make a "reasonable investigation" in support of them, which is a way of enlisting the grantors in the grantee's due diligence efforts. The representations and warranties are made as of the date of the grant. The covenant obligating the grantors to arrange for a cleanup, if that should ever be necessary, and the indemnity provisions of paragraph 8.6, extend into the future.[28]

---

28. For greater depth of treatment of CERCLA and hazardous waste liability, and its avoidance, generally, the reader is referred to the wealth of articles that have appeared on the subject in *Exchange* and *The Back Forty* over the past few years. *See, e.g.*, Matthew Ruyak, *From the Bench: CERCLA Update: Recent Court Decisions Interpreting Liability Provisions*, The Back Forty, March/April 1995, at 10; Thomas Haensly, *More Good News on CERCLA Liability for Easement Holders*, LTA Exchange, Winter 1995, at 17; Tara Mueller, *Court Holds Easement Holder Not Liable Under CERCLA*, The Back Forty, Nov./Dec. 1994, at 12; Thomas Haensly, *Limits on CERCLA Liability for Easement Holders*, LTA Exchange, Fall 1994, at 17; Soroush Shehabi, *Environmental Warranties and Indemnities*, The Back Forty, May/June 1994, at 8; Jacqueline Warren, *Indemnification: A Defense Against CERCLA Financial Responsibility*, LTA Exchange, Winter 1994, at 16; Andrew Bowman, *Anticipatory Release Upheld under CERCLA*, The Back Forty, Jul./Aug. 1993, at 17; Carol Boman, *CERCLA: New ASTM Standards for Environmental Site Assessments*, The Back Forty, May/June 1993, at 17; Ann Grimaldi, *Land Trust Directors and Officers: Coping with Personal Liability under CERCLA*, The Back Forty, July 1991, at 1; Jane Prohaska, *Courts Interpret "Owners" and "Operators" under CERCLA*, The Back Forty, Feb. 1991, at 7; Gail Secor, *Coping with Environmental Liability Risks in Land Trust Transactions*, The Back Forty, Feb. 1991, at 1; Tara Mueller, *Court Holds Landowner in Back-to-Back Transaction Not Liable under CERCLA*, The Back Forty, Dec. 90/Jan. 91, at 7; Rose Harvey and Mary Kearns-Kaplan, *Preventing Hazardous Waste Liability: Negotiating Strategies*, LTA Exchange, Summer 1989, at 10; Alison Kerester, *Environmental Due Diligence and Real Estate Transfers*, LTA Exchange, Summer 1989, at 4; Whitney Beals and Allen Morgen, *Toxic Waste—An Expensive Hazard to Land Trusts*, LTA Exchange, Summer 1989, at 13.

27. Hold Harmless (paragraph 8.6)

This clause is intended to ensure that none of the liabilities attendant on land ownership are inadvertently transferred with the easement. Unless the grantee takes on substantial management responsibilities with respect to the property, the grantee will have no direct control over any potential hazards, making it appropriate that the risk of these liabilities remain with the landowner. It is possible that the existence of the easement relationship or one or another of the easement's provisions might marginally increase the grantor's exposure, but particularly where self-help remedies are not provided, the additional risk is likely to be minuscule and the cost of insuring against it negligible. Typically, the grantor's risk, as landowner, is not enlarged at all by this provision. In contrast, the effect of these liabilities being borne by the grantee, multiplied over a substantial number of properties over which the grantee exercises no management control, could be devastating for the grantee's easement program, if not for its continuing existence as a viable organization. Nevertheless, in some areas of the country, a clause of this type might exceed the dictates of custom, particularly in a gift context. Grantees must determine for themselves whether there is any real danger of increased liability and the degree to which additional risk, if any, is acceptable.

The degree of public access provided by the easement is, of course, likely to influence how the risk is allocated. In some jurisdictions recreational use statutes are intended to protect landowners who permit public recreational access on their lands, but the scope of protection varies and is sometimes less than it seems.[29] Where substantial public access is contemplated, it may be appropriate for the grantee to assume the liabilities relating to it and indemnify the grantor. The following, which could be inserted as a separate paragraph following a paragraph designated as "Grantors' Hold Harmless," is a sample of a cross-indemnity where a public trail is created by an easement:

> **Grantee's Hold Harmless.** Grantee shall hold harmless, indemnify, and defend Grantors and their employees, agents, and contractors and the heirs, personal representatives, successors, and assigns of each of them (collectively, "Grantors' Indemnified Parties") from and against all liabilities, penalties, costs, losses, damages, expenses, causes of action, claims, demands, or judgments, including, without limitation, reasonable attorneys' fees, arising from or in any way connected with injury to or the death of any person, or physical damage to any property, resulting from any act, omission, condition, or other matter related to or occurring in, on, or about [a designated trail corridor], regardless of cause, unless due solely to the negligence of any of Grantors' Indemnified Parties.

Alternatively, whether or not a Grantee assumes any management responsibilities, a Grantee might simply give a cross-indemnity covering any and all of its activities on the property.

---

29. *See* note 22 for articles dealing with the vagaries of recreational use statutes.

The model provision requires the landowner not only to indemnify the grantee but to "defend" it. The purpose of this requirement is to put these matters in the landowner's hands from the inception of a claim, rather than waiting for any actual liability or loss to be determined. Some drafters expressly reserve a role for the grantee in choosing counsel. The provision is further enhanced by extending its protection to certain persons who may be exposed to liability by virtue of their special relationship to the grantee.

In addition to protecting the grantee against exposure to tort liability, the model provision indemnifies the grantee against the nontort liabilities of paragraphs 8.1 and 8.2 (liens and taxes), any breach of the covenants, representations, and warranties relating to environmental and general legal compliance contained in paragraphs 8.3 through 8.5, and hazardous waste and other potential liabilities relating to the property. As discussed in **comment 26 (Representations, Warranties, and Remediation)**, concern about these latter risks has become increasingly acute in recent years.

Indemnity clauses are not a substitute for insurance, and all easement holders should maintain adequate commercial general liability coverage.[30] As added protection, depending on the circumstances, it may be feasible for the grantee to be named as an "additional insured" on the landowner's policy.

28. Extinguishment (paragraph 9.1)

Absent state law to the contrary, the parties to an easement would normally be free to extinguish it by private mutual agreement. However, for a number of reasons, not the least of them being the public benefit at stake, a conservation easement holder is likely to resist extinguishment under all but the rarest of circumstances. Reflecting and reinforcing this posture, an easement qualifying under the IRS regulations may be extinguished, as the model provides, only by a judicial proceeding. *See* Treas. Reg. § 1.170A-14(g)(6)(i).

Section 1.170A-14(g)(6)(i) of the IRS regulations describes the circumstances that might justify extinguishment as involving a "change in conditions surrounding the property" that makes the conservation purpose of the easement "impossible or impractical" to achieve. The drafter should be aware, though, that these are loaded terms in property law. Under the traditional rule, easements can be terminated only if their purpose becomes "impossible" to accomplish. In jurisdictions following the traditional rule, the so-called "changed conditions" doctrine referred to in the IRS regulations applies not to easements but to restrictive covenants and equitable servitudes. The changed conditions doctrine sets a lower threshold for extinguishment, as the IRS's somewhat loose use of the term "impractical" might suggest. It may, for example, be used to terminate a restriction on grounds of economic hardship. Under that rubric, changes in the neighborhood of a restricted property that greatly increased the property's value for prohibited uses or

---

30. *Editor's note:* The Land Trust Alliance offers land trusts access to an insurance program designed especially for land trusts and their land conservation programs through membership in the Alliance.

decreased its value for permitted uses could be enough to compel termination. Of course, the circumstance most likely to bring about this state of affairs is acute development pressure, precisely the circumstance under which the open space protected by a conservation easement is likely to become most strategically important.

The Uniform Conservation Easement Act specifically provides that a conservation easement may be terminated "in the same manner as other *easements*," presumably foreclosing application of the changed conditions doctrine in those states adopting the Act that have confined the doctrine to the context of restrictive covenants and equitable servitudes.[31] Some states have addressed the issue head-on by statute.[32] The model assumes that the impossibility standard is the correct one to apply to conservation easements, taking pains to avoid the introduction of ambiguous terms. Whether the courts will agree remains to be seen. In practice, the applicable standard is likely to vary from state to state.[33]

On the theory that a court will give weight to the intent of the original parties on the question, some drafters add language to indicate that economic hardship has been considered and rejected as a potential ground for termination. The following sample, which, as the bracketed portion shows, can be adjusted to be more or less severe in tone, could be inserted as a separate paragraph after paragraph 9.1 of the model:

> **Economic Hardship.** In making this grant, Grantors have considered the possibility that uses prohibited by the terms of this Easement may become more economically valuable than permitted uses, and that neighboring properties may in the future be put entirely to such prohibited uses. It is the intent of both Grantors and Grantee that any such changes shall not be deemed to be circumstances justifying the termination or extinguishment of this Easement pursuant to paragraph 9.1. [In addition, the inability of Grantors, or their heirs, successors, or assigns, to conduct or implement any or all of the uses permitted under the terms of this Easement, or the unprofitability of doing so, shall not impair the validity of this Easement or be considered grounds for its termination or extinguishment pursuant to paragraph 9.1.]

Technical distinctions aside, the outcome in an extinguishment proceeding should turn on consideration of the public benefit involved. A strong argument can be made that where the public purpose of a conservation easement has continuing vitality, economic hardship should not be a factor. The important point, from a drafting perspective, is that the range of purposes served by an easement

---

31. *See* Unif. Conservation Easement Act § 2(a), 12 U.L.A. 65 (emphasis added).

32. *See, e.g.,* Me. Rev. Stat. Ann. tit. 33 § 478 (West Supp. 1986); Iowa Code Ann. § 111D.2 (West 1984).

33. Note, Jeffrey A. Blackie, *Conservation Easements and the Doctrine of Changed Conditions*, 40 Hastings L.J. 1187 (1989); *see also* Gerald Korngold, *Privately Held Conservation Servitudes: A Policy Analysis in the Context of In Gross Real Covenants and Easements*, 63 Tex L. Rev. 433 (1984); Barrett and Livermore, *The Conservation Easement in California*, 32-34, 117-118; Powell, *The Law of Real Property*, § 34A.07.

must be clearly stated. Often conservation easements serve purposes that are both broad (*e.g.*, a community's need for open space) and narrow (*e.g.*, preservation of endangered species habitat). Care should be taken to express the full range of purposes in the easement so that the impossibility of fulfilling a narrow purpose (resulting, for example, from the extinction of a species) will not be allowed to defeat a broader purpose.

One form of extinguishment not treated in the model is that which would result from the merger of the easement with the underlying fee in the event the grantee were ever to become the owner of the property. (In some states, where merger doctrine may be modified by statutes dealing with charitable uses, merger may not be automatic.) Under some circumstances, landowners might be concerned that merger could result in the frustration of their original intent in granting an easement. They might be concerned that a land trust, strapped for cash, might sell off the property free of restrictions, for example, or that a governmental grantee might use it for some other purpose, like a school site. Where merger has been a concern, a number of approaches have been used to attempt to avoid it. The most common, perhaps, is a simple statement of intent, such as the following:

> **Merger.** Grantors and Grantee agree that the terms of this Easement shall survive any merger of the fee and easement interests in the Property.

Another is to have the grantee covenant to immediately convey a new easement to a new grantee or to reserve an easement upon subsequent transfer of the fee. The effectiveness of such methods is yet to be tested. Alternatively, in jurisdictions where it is valid, an executory limitation, like the one set out in the supplementary paragraphs, might be enlarged to include the grantee's acquisition of the fee as a triggering event. Of course, in some situations the grantee's acquisition of complete control over the property, which enhances its ability to assure that the land is optimally managed for conservation purposes, will be viewed as desirable, and no mechanism to prevent merger will be necessary.

One concern that has been expressed with respect to the possibility of merger is that, because it affects the perpetuity of an easement, it might raise doubts about deductibility under federal tax law. This concern seems overblown. Merger is only one of many remote possibilities that can affect an easement; to try to provide for all of them is to engage in an exercise in futility. The IRS recognizes this, stating in the regulations that where the possibility of some future act or event occurring is "so remote as to be negligible," it can safely be disregarded. (*See* Treas. Reg. § 1.170A-14(g)(3), which cites as an example the failure to rerecord the easement every 30 years as required by a state marketable title statute.) In most cases the possibility of merger, it is submitted, will fall squarely within this rubric. What effect the doctrine of merger might have on deductibility when the possibility of merger is certain or near certain (for example, where a remainder or testamentary gift to the grantee is contemplated at the time of the easement grant) is another question—one that has not been authoritatively answered to date.[34]

---

34. For a rare discussion of the subject in a tax planning context see Small, *The Federal Tax Law of Conservation Easements*, E-3, E-5.

Finally, the possibility of merger should not cause an easement to run afoul of a perpetuity requirement under state law, as long as the easement instrument expressly provides for a perpetual term.[35]

29. Valuation (paragraph 9.2)

This provision meets the requirements of Section 1.17OA-14(g)(6)(ii) of the tax regulations, which provides that the grantee is entitled to a share of the proceeds of a sale, exchange, or involuntary conversion of the property following extinguishment of an easement "at least equal to the proportionate value that the...conservation restriction at the time of the gift bears to the property as a whole at that time." Although the regulations might be interpreted to require no more than a personal side agreement between the original donor and donee regarding the division of proceeds upon extinguishment, the universal practice has been to provide for this in the easement document itself. Many practitioners employ the same device even where a tax deductible gift is not involved. (Note the bracketed portions for addition or deletion as appropriate.)

The policy behind the IRS requirement is to assure that the public receive fair value for the tax benefit bestowed even if the easement should be extinguished in the future. Grantee organizations, understandably, have embraced the provision. Practitioners should be alert to one potential problem, however. The IRS requires that the ratio of the value of the easement to the value of the property unencumbered by the easement remain constant over the life of the easement. But, of course, the value of the development rights of a property, and thus the theoretical value of the easement, could go up or down over time for any number of reasons, including, for example, zoning changes or a shift in local development patterns, or even the conveyance of other easements in the area. Where the value of the development rights did change substantially, a division of proceeds according to the artificially fixed formula of this provision might prove unfair.

The IRS makes no allowance for appreciation due to improvements, although an allocation similar to that in the model provision is certainly called for as a matter of basic fairness. Similarly, the possibility that senior claims might exist should be acknowledged and a mechanism for deducting the amount of such claims provided. Provision for the deduction of costs might also be made.

One further potential complication is the fact that, in the case of a gift, the correct ratio for determining the parties' proportionate share may not be known at the time of the grant. Moreover, the ratio will not become final, technically speaking, until the statute of limitations for the gift (three years) has run. One way to deal with this is to require the parties to amend the easement to set forth the ratio when known. Another is to provide that the parties will execute an

---

35. For discussion of merger in greater depth, see Paul Doscher and Sylvia Bates, *Merging Ownership of Conservation Easements with Fee Interests: The Experience of the Society for the Protection of New Hampshire Forests*, The Back Forty, August 1991, at 1 and William Ginsberg, *The Destructibility of Conservation Easements Through Merger*, The Back Forty, *id.*, at 5.

acknowledgement form stating the appropriate ratio, when known, to be kept on file with Grantee, and agree to amend it, if necessary, to conform to any contrary final determination of the IRS or court of competent jurisdiction.

Finally, the mechanics of enforcing this provision may prove complicated, perhaps requiring the imposition, following extinguishment, of a lien for the stipulated proportionate value of the easement, which presumably would be due on sale. Some drafters attempt to provide for this ahead of time by stating that the terms of the extinguishment section will survive extinguishment and constitute a lien on the property. If the event subsequent to extinguishment is an "exchange" rather than a sale or involuntary conversion, an expectation of "cashing out" may not be realistic.

Where an easement is purchased rather than donated, or where qualification under I.R.C. § 170(h) for income, gift, or estate tax purposes is otherwise not a factor, the parties are, of course, free to deal with extinguishment in any way they see fit, subject only to whatever constraints may exist under state law.

30. Condemnation (paragraph 9.3)

The IRS requirement for the allocation of proceeds is triggered by extinguishment under the "impossibility" or "changed conditions" doctrine, whichever is applicable to easements in a given jurisdiction, and subsequent sale of the property in question. Condemnation is an entirely separate method of extinguishment, with its own set of governing laws. Nevertheless, most drafters attempt to apply a proceeds allocation rule similar to the model's to condemnation.

Although the law varies from jurisdiction to jurisdiction, the majority rule is that easements represent a compensable property interest.[36] While case law is scarce, there is also precedent for valuing an easement in gross the way the IRS does, according to its negative effect on the value of the property as a whole.[37] In some jurisdictions, however, the property's compensable value may be limited to its restricted value, in which case a proportionate allocation would be unfair to the landowner, while the alternative—no allocation—would be unfair to the grantee. Some drafters attempt to head off this problem by resorting to a so-called "self-destruction" or *"in terrorem"* clause, privately canceling the easement in the face of a taking. At least one commentator has counselled against this approach, however, suggesting that it may undercut attempts to challenge the taking, while operating as a waiver of a grantee's potential claim for damages.[38]

---

36. See Gregory Bialecki, *What Must the Taking Authority Pay for Land Subject to a Conservation Easement?*, The Back Forty, July-August 1990, at 6.)

37. See *Hartford National Bank and Trust Company v. Redevelopment Agency of City of Bristol*, 164 Conn. 337, 321 A.2d 469 (1973); see also discussion in Gregory Bialecki, *Eminent Domain Takings of Land Subject to Conservation Easements*, The Back Forty, September 1990, at 8.

38. See Bialecki, *Eminent Domain Takings of Land Subject to Conservation Easements*, note 35, at 9. For an unsuccessful attempt by the IRS to use a "self-destruction" or *"in terrorem"* clause as a grounds for challenging the deductibility of an easement, see *Stotler et al. v. Commissioner*, 53 T.C.M. (CCH) 973 (1987).

Such a clause should be used only after a careful analysis of its likely effect in a given jurisdiction.

One further wrinkle. In order to prevent protected properties from becoming easy targets for condemnation, conservation easement statutes in some states expressly provide that, in the event of condemnation, the landowner is entitled to be compensated for the full value of the property without regard to the easement.[39] Where the condemning authority and the grantee are coordinate governmental agencies, the policy behind this kind of statutory proviso is likely to be well-served by it. Where an independent nonprofit organization is the grantee, however, it may overshoot the mark. Assuming the parties are free to bargain for an allocation between themselves—an assumption that is yet to be tested in this context—a provision like the model's would serve to protect the grantee's interests. In some jurisdictions, property put to one public use may not be diverted to another inconsistent public use without legislative approval. This "prior public use" doctrine is another way of dealing with the easy-target problem, without infringing the grantee's rights.

There are likely to be circumstances where condemnation will affect the parties' interests to different degrees. There are also likely to be situations where application of a predetermined formula for allocating proceeds will prove unfair. Drafters might consider providing for reappraisal to address these concerns.

31. Application of Proceeds (paragraph 9.4)

The IRS regulations require that the grantee's use of the proceeds it receives as the result of an extinguishment be "consistent with the conservation purposes" of the grant. *See* Treas. Reg. § 1.170A-14(g)(6)(1). Presumably, it is sufficient that the proceeds be applied to any conservation purpose of the grantee organization in the broadest sense, which for conservation organizations would include general operations.

32. Assignment (paragraph 10)

The model restriction on transfer complies with a requirement of the IRS regulations. *See* Treas. Reg. § 1.170A-14(c)(2). This provision is also important for assuring continuing qualification under any applicable state law.

Some easements require the grantor's consent to an assignment, but circumstances might arise that could make such a requirement sticky, if not with the grantor then with subsequent owners. In any case, unless carefully limited, the enforceability of such a restraint could be questioned. To avoid problems the model allows the grantee to assign freely to any qualified organization, which, as defined by the IRS, includes governmental agencies. If a grantor has particular concerns on the subject (for example, a preference for certain organizations or reservations about others), this provision could be linked to an executory

---

39. *See* Cal. Gov't. Code § 51095 for an example under California law.

limitation, such as the one set out in the supplementary paragraphs, and the list of designated back-up grantees could be lengthened.

The IRS regulations state that the grantee must, as a "condition" of transfer, require that a transferee continue to carry out the conservation purposes of the grant. Although the regulations are unclear on the point, it is unlikely that the reservation of a reversionary interest by the original grantee is necessary to satisfy this requirement. In practice, most organizations prefer to avoid retaining a reversionary interest upon assignment.

If the grantor endows a monitoring fund at the time of the grant, it may be appropriate to provide for its transfer along with the easement.

33. Subsequent Transfers (paragraph 11)

Recording the easement is sufficient in virtually all jurisdictions to put any subsequent transferees of the fee or other interests in the property on constructive notice of the easement and to bind them to its terms. Paragraph 11 is included in the easement not because it is strictly necessary but as a practical means of increasing the likelihood that future purchasers, encumbrancers, or lessees will have *actual* notice of the easement ahead of any transfer. By requiring the grantor to notify the grantee it is also intended to afford the grantee an opportunity to educate the transferee regarding the easement. Some drafters add a requirement that the easement be appended to the purchase and sale contract as well.[40]

Experience to date indicates that the provision may be honored in the breach as often as not. If permissible under state law, recording a request for notice of transfer would serve to alleviate the problem.

Some easements include a right of first refusal in favor of the grantee, providing it a preemptive right to buy the property in the event the grantor decides to sell. Whether such a right can run with the land in perpetuity, however, is doubtful.

34. Estoppel Certificates (paragraph 12)

Potential lenders and buyers are likely to require proof of the landowner's compliance with the easement, and this provision requires the grantee to certify the landowner's good standing upon request. Violations of which the Grantee has no knowledge, such as latent or concealed violations, are excepted.

35. Notices (paragraph 13)

Although the model does not require it, if delivery cannot be made in person, certified mail (return receipt requested) is recommended whenever proof of

---

40. Landowners who fail to give purchasers notice of a conservation easement could lose a sale on account of it. *See Fenster v. Hadi*, 1991 WL 257295 (Conn. Super.) (1991), where the failure to list a conservation easement with other encumbrances in a purchase agreement was grounds for rescission.

receipt is necessary to determine the relevant dates for the running of any time period triggered by notice. When notice is deemed to have been delivered for purposes of triggering any stated time period is a matter of state law, although the parties can stipulate what constitutes delivery, as, by way of one example, the following does:

> ...All notices shall be deemed delivered and effective upon actual receipt if given personally or by private courier or upon deposit with the U.S. Postal Service if given by mail.

Provision for fax transmittal might also be made.

Where the addresses given in the caption at the beginning of the easement agree with the addresses designated for notice, they need only be referenced rather than restated here.

36. Recordation (paragraph 14)

Recordation is the only way to put the world at large on constructive notice of a conservation easement. It is required by many state easement enabling statutes and, for all practical purposes, by the IRS. *See* Treas. Reg. § 1.170A-14(g)(1).[41] Rerecording an easement may be required after a prescribed period of years under the marketable title acts that have been passed in some states to clear land titles of dormant interests.

37. General Provisions (paragraphs 15.1-15.10)

To a limited extent the parties can guide the courts in the interpretation of the easement, particularly with respect to the application of general rules of construction, and these general provisions, by and large, are included for that purpose. Many of them are standard terms, routinely included in substantial written agreements. They are, for the most part, self-explanatory.

Paragraph 15.2. State easement statutes might provide independent support for liberal construction of an easement, and if so, paragraph 15.2 should be keyed to them.

Paragraph 15.3. The "no forfeiture" clause is included to enable title insurers to provide coverage to this effect—something routinely required by mortgage lenders.

Paragraph 15.6 provides that grantors are liable under the easement both collectively and individually.

Paragraphs 15.7 and 15.8. Since an easement runs with the land (paragraph 15.7), an express provision for terminating the parties' rights and obligations upon transfer may seem superfluous. It is included here (paragraph 15.8), however, to make it clear that liability for acts or omissions occurring prior to transfer does *not* terminate upon transfer.

---

41. *See also Satullo v. Commissioner*, 66 T.C.M. (CCH) 1697 (1993), where failure to record an easement in a timely manner in accordance with state law was fatal to a claimed deduction.

Paragraph 15.10 is included to enable either party, as a matter of convenience, to submit its copy of the easement as the original in a judicial proceeding.

Finally, practitioners should be alert to the possibility that a grantor might propose inserting a provision for termination of the easement in the event a federal tax deduction for the donation is denied. The validity of this kind of condition is, under an established line of tax cases, problematic at best.[42] In any case, there is the danger that by calling into question the grantor's "donative intent," which is a prerequisite to deductibility, such a provision could become self-fulfilling. The proper way to resolve any substantial doubt about the deductibility of a proposed conservation easement gift is to seek an opinion from experienced counsel—or, in unusual cases, a private letter ruling from the IRS—before making the donation.

38. Habendum Clause

"To have and to hold...etc...." (*"habendum et tenendum,"* in Latin) is traditional, though not universally required, language for concluding a grant. As in the grant clause, care must be taken to choose language that complies with the conveyancing requirements of the jurisdiction in which the property is located. Among other things, a statement of delivery may be required.

39. Signatures, Acknowledgements, and Exhibits

This form conservation easement, like a lease, is not only a conveyance but also a contract, intended to bind both parties by its terms. Consequently, it is structured as a two-party deed, called an indenture, to be signed by both the grantor and grantee. Besides the grantor and grantee, additional signatories might include any state or local agency whose approval of the easement may be required by applicable law, the preparer of the easement (required in some jurisdictions), and the designated back-up grantee, if any. Corporate officers, whose authority to bind a corporation is prescribed by state law as well as the corporation's bylaws, may be required to affix their corporate seal in some states. Acknowledgment of the signatures by a notary—or, in some jurisdictions, a justice of the peace—is a prerequisite to recordation of a document in most state. Exhibits are attached immediately following the signature pages.

40. Supplementary Provisions

The designation of the provisions that follow as "supplementary" is not meant to imply that everything that has come before is essential but only that a decision to include one or more of these provisions in an easement is likely to turn more on particular facts, or involve stronger preferences, than the provisions that have already been discussed.

---

42. See *Commissioner v. Procter*, 142 F.2d 824 (1944); *Ward v. Commissioner*, 87 T.C. 78 (1986).

41. Arbitration (supplementary paragraph 5.3)

It is impossible to anticipate every potential problem in an agreement intended, theoretically, to endure forever. Disputes are bound to arise, and some mechanism must be provided for their resolution. Increasingly in recent years, arbitration has been viewed as an attractive alternative to resorting to the courts. Many see it as a cheaper, faster, and somehow less threatening, even gentler, means of settling differences—a kind of soft path to reconciliation. That image may or may not square with reality in particular cases. It is important to realize that arbitration is not the equivalent of mediation or counseling. It can be every bit as adversarial as trial, and depending on the issues, it can be equally if not more consuming of the time and resources of the parties and their attorneys. It is true that, whereas access to the courts can be substantially delayed, the availability of arbitrators is almost immediate. But if the issues to be heard are complex, the relatively relaxed rules of arbitration (little or no pre-hearing discovery and few if any restrictions on the admissibility of evidence) can prolong the matter painfully, and unlike judges, arbitrators are paid by the parties.

Arbitration is absolutely inadequate in circumstances where an injunction is required; only the courts have the power to provide such relief, and in at least this one area they act with dispatch. A temporary restraining order, for example, can be issued immediately upon the application of one party even before the other party has had the opportunity to appear and oppose it. But the courts' extraordinary powers extend beyond their ability to issue injunctions and include, among other things, the authority to impose sanctions where appropriate and a broad latitude to fashion meaningful remedies. In the easement context this could be of great importance, particularly where a "creative" approach to the issue of damages, including punitive or exemplary damages, is needed. Conservation values are hard to express in monetary terms, but easement holders, encouraged in some jurisdictions by liberal state statutes, will want to establish standards of compensation for the loss of aesthetic or "quality of life" values. For this, of course, the courts are indispensable. Equally important, whereas arbitration may settle a dispute, it does not make law, and the creation of favorable precedent through the careful and selective judicial enforcement of conservation easements will be a matter of great significance for easement programs nationwide. It also should be pointed out that arbitrators have no enforcement powers; resort to the courts is still necessary to confirm and enforce an arbitrator's award against a recalcitrant loser.

In short, although arbitration has its virtues, it is no panacea. For relatively simple disputes involving questions that can be easily stated and that call for straightforward answers, arbitration may be appropriate. For more complicated matters, which could benefit from either the focusing that modern litigation, for all its faults, demands or the application of a court's plenary powers, arbitration can be a poor choice.

The model sets forth a typical arbitration provision but intentionally limits its scope to the kind of dispute for which it is most suited in the easement context:

prospective application of the consistency test. The parties may choose to expand its applicability to other contexts as they deem appropriate for their particular circumstances. Of course, whatever the easement provides, the parties remain free to submit any disagreement to arbitration at any time by mutual consent.

The procedure established in the model encourages the parties to agree on the selection of a single arbitrator. Both parties should recognize that this is in their best interest, not only for controlling costs but also for ensuring that the matter proceeds expeditiously (simplified scheduling) and efficiently (it is easier to educate one person than three). As for the choice of rules to govern the proceedings, the drafter has a number of sources to consult, including the American Arbitration Association or other arbitration association rules and, in some jurisdictions, statutory rules.

As always, of course, drafters should consult local law to determine whether there are any specific requirements regarding contractual arbitration clauses peculiar to the jurisdiction in question. Some jurisdictions, for example, may require notice on the front of the contract that disputes are subject to arbitration.

42. Mediation (supplementary paragraph 5.3)

Alternative dispute resolution has become a growth industry in recent years, and mediation is at the heart of it. Whereas, broadly speaking, litigation, and even, for the most part, arbitration, is designed to determine who is right and who is wrong in a given dispute—to produce a winner and a loser—mediation is designed to approach disputes as problems to be solved by the parties through mutual effort—a joint search for a solution that is at least satisfactory to both sides. When the parties enter into mediation in good faith, with the intention of really working hard to resolve their differences, the process can prove not only effective but enlightening. Of course, the skill and knowledge of the mediator can be critical. The good ones bring an understanding of the anatomy of disputes to the table that enables them to see things that the parties may be blind to, including obstacles blocking the paths to potential solutions that need not be unmovable. If a dispute might be susceptible to resolution by mediation, the parties would do well to find that out. As anyone who has been through it knows, litigation is something to be avoided if at all possible.

The model mediation provision, which might be used instead of an arbitration provision, loosely follows the federal court mediation guidelines. It is mandatory within its limited range, which is identical to that of the arbitration provision: disputes over proposed activities from which the grantor agrees to refrain pending the course of the resolution process. The process is not binding, however; a party can drop out after a stated period, such as ninety days from inception. The time period provided is intentionally modest. If the parties cannot make mediation work for them, they are likely to know it within relatively short order. Again, the parties are always free to enlarge the scope or time period by mutual agreement.

43. Amendment (supplementary paragraph between 9 and 10)

Until quite recently, most conservation easements have been silent regarding amendment, at least in part to avoid encouraging the notion that their terms can be easily changed. It is unrealistic to think, however, that the need to amend will never arise. Because easements are perpetual, there are bound to be changed circumstances over time that require amendment—at least in a substantial number of cases—and many consider it prudent to set the ground rules ahead of time. In some states, unless amendment is expressly provided for, the supervision of a court is necessary to modify an easement. In others, the approval of one or more governmental agencies may be required. It is possible too, in some states, that, however inapt, trust law considerations might creep into the picture, raising questions about the intent of the original donor.

To prevent the model provision from raising any question about the deductibility of a donated easement or the qualification of the grantee or the easement under any applicable law, a restriction on amendment is provided with reference to state law and Section 170(h) of the Internal Revenue Code. Absent fraud, the IRS's interest in a particular gift ends when the statute of limitations has run. However, its interest in the affairs of the tax-exempt grantee continues for as long as the grantee exists, so the requirements of the tax code and regulations remain relevant to the amendment issue long after the grant. It is possible, of course, that an amendment could affect the valuation of an easement for tax purposes, in which case it would be the donor's responsibility, if still the landowner, to report the recovery of any amount previously deducted.[43] Some organizations will not permit an amendment that would decrease the reported value of the easement. Others require a *quid pro quo* designed to yield a net benefit on the conservation side of the account. Still others will not permit any additional development or improvements. Beyond the differences in detail of their amendment policies, however, it is safe to say that the overwhelming consensus among land conservation organizations is that an amendment must never be permitted to diminish the conservation values of the property involved.

Most practitioners would counsel that the right to amend be used sparingly and, especially where an area-wide easement program is in effect, equitably (like properties should be treated alike). The impact of an amendment goes beyond the easement at hand; it can affect an organization's entire program, as well as the attitude of the courts, the IRS, and state and local legislatures toward conservation easements. Great care should be taken to see that the consistency requirement of this paragraph is not allowed to become an empty one. If an amendment is inconsistent with the purpose of the easement, its validity—or worse, the validity of the easement as a whole—may be called into question.

---

43. This is the so-called "tax benefit rule." *See Alice Phelan Sullivan Corporation v. United States*, 381 F.2d 399 (1967); Rev. Rul. 76-150, 1976-1 C.B. 38.

44. Executory Limitation (supplementary paragraph between 10 and 11)

"Executory limitation" is the legal term used to describe the creation of a future interest in real property in favor of a third party. Although under normal circumstances an open-ended executory interest would violate the common law rule against perpetuities, which prohibits the creation of interests that may not become vested until the remote future, a grant to a charitable organization followed by a limitation to another charitable organization constitutes, in most jurisdictions, an exception to the rule.[44] Some easements provide a detailed list of potential future grantees stated in order of preference. The model indicates the basic approach. An alternative would be simply to provide that the grantee will choose a successor if any of the events specified occurs.

Of the triggering events, qualification under Section 170(h) of the Internal Revenue Code is the least important over the long term since the adverse consequences of a failure to qualify disappear after the statute of limitations has run with respect to the gift. Some easements add that the grantee's failure to enforce the easement will trigger the limitation. What constitutes a failure to enforce is open to interpretation, however, and for obvious reasons a limitation of this type works better if there is no room for doubt that the triggering event has occurred. In any case, it should be remembered that, in most jurisdictions, the attorney general of the state where the property is located has authority to assure that the easement is enforced.

Although, theoretically, the transfer effected by an executory limitation is automatic upon occurrence of the triggering event, in practice a quiet title action may be necessary to confirm the back-up grantee's interest. The ultimate back-up to the easement, as the model illustrates, is provided by the courts. If a back-up grantee is to be designated, its consent to the designation should be obtained beforehand, which might be evidenced by its signing the easement at its inception. As with an assignment, provision for transfer of any monitoring fund may be appropriate.

In addition to, or instead of, an executory limitation, some easements provide for back-up enforcement by another organization without divesting the holder. This can be done through a co-grantee arrangement or a limited power of enforcement to be exercised under specified conditions, including, for example, the primary grantee's inability or refusal to enforce the easement.[45] The practice, common in some areas, calls for care in establishing ground rules for the relationship, which, in the co-grantee arrangement, is likely to extend beyond enforcement to discretionary approvals and monitoring duties. A separate memorandum of understanding is often the best way to accomplish this.

---

44. For a discussion of executory limitations and defeasible grants in general see Barrett and Livermore, *The Conservation Easement in California*, 95-101.

45. The Uniform Conservation Easement Act countenances the explicit creation of third-party enforcement rights in an easement. *See* Unif. Conservation Easement Act § § 1(3) & 3(a)(4), 12 U.L.A. 65. *See* also Tad Ames and Douglas Muir, *Conservation Easement Partnerships in the Northeast*, LTA Exchange, Spring 1995, at 8.

Although beyond the scope of this discussion, practitioners should be alert to the possibility that non-contractual third-party enforcement rights have been or may be recognized by statute or case law in their jurisdiction. Such rights may be vested in abutting landowners or the public at large as ultimate beneficiaries of the easement.[46]

45. Subordination (supplementary paragraph between 10 and 11)

Foreclosure of a prior mortgage or deed of trust would extinguish an easement. Consequently, for a qualified conservation contribution, the IRS requires existing mortgage holders to subordinate their rights to "the right of the qualified organization to enforce the conservation purposes of the gift in perpetuity." *See* Treas. Reg. § 1.170A-14(g)(2).

A mortgage lender's interest in a property is, of course, as security for a debt. Because a conservation easement may significantly reduce the market value of a property, it may be difficult to get a lender to enter into a subordination agreement. Unless the lender can be assured that the value of its security interest will continue to be adequate, and that its ability to realize the debt from it, if necessary, will not be impaired by the Easement, the lender will not agree to subordinate. Even where a lender's margin of security is ample, unfamiliarity with conservation easements may represent an additional barrier to be overcome. Often subordination negotiations begin as an exercise in educating the lender about the nature of conservation easements—the scope of rights and responsibilities involved. The process can be a protracted one. Nevertheless, a number of land trusts have success stories to share.[47]

Assuming sufficient value remains in a given property to secure an outstanding loan, a limited subordination on terms similar to those stated in the following sample subordination agreement should go a long way toward satisfying the legitimate concerns of a hesitant lender. Although untested to date, because it assures that the easement will be enforceable in perpetuity, it should also meet the IRS requirement.

---

46. For example, in Illinois, abutting landowners, landowners within 500 feet of the burdened property, the state, and any unit of local government has standing to enforce an easement. *See* Ill. Ann. Stat. ch. 765, para. 120/4 (Smith-Hurd 1995). Elsewhere, in at least two cases, third-party standing has been denied. *See Friends of Shawangunks, Inc. v. Knowlton*, 64 N.Y.2d 387, 476 N.E.2d 988 (1985); *Knowles v. Codex Corp.*, 12 Mass. App. 493, 426 N.E.2d 734 (1981). For a discussion of a trend toward expansion of the public's right of standing and how it might relate to conservation easements, see Hussein Saffouri, *Conservation Easements and Third-Party Enforcement*, The Back Forty, January-February 1995, at 16.

47. *See, e.g.*, Bill Long, *Negotiating a Subordination Agreement*, LTA Exchange, Spring 1989, at 8; Betty Wiechec, *Subordinating Mortgages to Conservation Easements*, LTA Exchange, Fall 1986, at 14.

SUBORDINATION AGREEMENT

This Agreement is entered into by and among __[Lender]__ , a __[state of incorporation]__ corporation with its principal office located at _____ _____ ("Mortgagee"); __[Land owners]__ , whose mailing address is _____ ("Mortgagors"); and __[Land Trust]__ , a non-profit __[state of incorporation]__ corporation, with its principal office located at _____ ("Land Trust").

WHEREAS, Mortgagors are the owners of that certain real property in _____ County, __[state]__ described in Exhibit A attached hereto and incorporated by this reference ("Property"); and

WHEREAS, Mortgagee is the holder of a promissory note made by Mortgagors, dated _____, in the original principal amount of _____ ("Note"), which is secured by a mortgage encumbering the Property of even date therewith, recorded on __[date]__ , at Volume ____ of Mortgages, Page ____, Records of _____ County, __[state]__ , a copy of which is attached hereto as Exhibit B and incorporated by this reference ("Mortgage"); and

WHEREAS, concurrently with this agreement, Mortgagors are conveying a conservation easement over the Property to Land Trust, which is more particularly described in Exhibit C attached hereto and incorporated by this reference ("Easement"); and

WHEREAS, upon Mortgagors' request, Mortgagee has consented to subordinate the Mortgage to the terms of the Easement, which Mortgagee has reviewed and approved; and

WHEREAS, the Easement, which would not otherwise be conveyed by Mortgagors nor accepted by Land Trust, is being conveyed and accepted in reliance on this agreement;

NOW THEREFORE, in consideration of the above and the mutual covenants and promises contained herein, and other valuable consideration the receipt and sufficiency of which is hereby acknowledged, it is represented and agreed as follows:

1. The Mortgage is subordinated and hereafter shall be junior to the Easement to the extent necessary to permit Land Trust to enforce the purpose of the Easement in perpetuity and to prevent any modification or extinguishment of the Easement by the exercise of any right of Mortgagee.

2. The priority of the Mortgage with respect to any valid claim on the part of Mortgagee to the proceeds of any sale, condemnation proceedings, or insurance, or to the leases, rents, and profits of the Property, is not affected hereby, and any lien that may be created by Land Trust's exercise of any of its rights under the Easement shall be junior to the Mortgage; provided, however, that if the Easement is terminated under the circumstances described in

section 9 of the Easement, Land Trust shall be entitled to compensation in accordance with the terms set forth therein.

3. Mortgagee shall not be joined as a defendant in any action to enforce the easement seeking damages, fees, or costs of any kind, and the Mortgage shall have priority over any judgment entered for any costs, fees, or damages under the Easement, unless the violation representing the grounds for the action was caused by Mortgagee or its agents or employees.

4. If at any time in an action to enforce the Easement Land Trust obtains injunctive relief requiring that the Property be restored in any respect, Mortgagee shall not be held liable for any costs of restoration, regardless of who is in possession of the Property, unless Mortgagee or its agents or employees is responsible for the condition requiring restoration.

5. In the event of the foreclosure of the Mortgage, whether by judicial decree or pursuant to a power of sale, the Easement shall not be extinguished but shall survive and continue to encumber the Property.

6. This agreement shall be binding upon, and inure to the benefit of, the parties hereto and their respective personal representatives, heirs, successors, and assigns.

7. An endorsement has been placed upon the Note stating that it has, by this instrument, been subordinated to the Easement to the extent described herein.

8. This agreement shall be recorded immediately after the Easement.

Entered into this _____ day of _____, _____.

Mortgagee _____
by _____
its _____ [official capacity] _____

Mortgagors _____
_____

Land Trust _____
by _____
its _____ [official capacity] _____

[Acknowledgments]

SCHEDULE OF EXHIBITS

A. Legal Description of Property

B. Copy of Mortgage

C. Identification of Conservation Easement

A lender may have other concerns in addition to those set forth, and the parties should make every effort to satisfy them. Possible additional concerns might include the right to rebuild structures in the event of a casualty loss; the extent of reserved development rights; public access, if any; and, perhaps, notice and an opportunity to cure a landowner's default under the easement.

A lender might also balk at the model's provision for the division of proceeds following extinguishment or condemnation (section 9), which the sample subordination agreement addresses in paragraph 2. Whether Treas. Reg. § 1.170A-14(g)(2) requires the subordination to this provision is an open question. Since the grantee's right *to enforce* the easement is not implicated, some practitioners consider it negotiable. Others would argue, at least with respect to extinguishment, that the division of proceeds requirement is what allows "the conservation purpose" of the grant to "nonetheless be treated as protected in perpetuity" in the eyes of the IRS, and a lender must therefore subordinate to it. *See* Treas. Reg. § 1.170A-14(g)(6).

As always, the form the agreement takes will depend heavily on the law of the jurisdiction involved. In some states, for example, specific statutory notice language might be required at the beginning of the document.

It is not technically necessary to refer to a concurrent mortgage subordination in the easement document itself. Some drafters prefer to do so, however, in the interest of making the easement a convenient single source of reference, and the model supplementary paragraph is reflective of that practice.

Of course, the sample agreement above assumes a lender who has expressed concerns that must be addressed in order to win its consent to a subordination. Under some circumstances, the parties may find that a lender has no reservations about executing a broad form subordination. In that case, subject to the requirements of local law, a simple subordination clause, like the sample below, might well be added to the easement itself, which the lender—and in the case of a deed of trust, the trustee—must then sign to evidence its consent. Again, as stated in the limited subordination agreement, the underlying promissory note should be endorsed to reflect the subordination.

Subordination. _____ ("Mortgagee") is the holder of a certain promissory note made by Grantors, dated _____, which is secured by a mortgage encumbering the Property of even date therewith, recorded on _____, at Volume ____ of Mortgages, Page ____, Records of _____ County, [state] , [a copy of which is attached hereto as Exhibit ____ and incorporated by this reference] ("Mortgage"). Mortgagee hereby consents to the terms and intent of this Easement and intentionally and unconditionally agrees that the lien of the Mortgage is subordinated and hereafter shall be junior to this Easement.

There is another potential reason to deal with subordination in the easement: to set the terms for possible future partial subordination of the *easement* for the benefit of future lenders. The long-term viability of an easement is likely to be weakened to the extent the easement interferes unnecessarily with the grantor's or the grantor's successors' ability to obtain adequate mortgage financing—whether for land, improvements, or equipment—in the future. As long as the IRS's standard for existing mortgages is met, and the grantee's right to enforce the easement in perpetuity is preserved, a provision dealing with partial subordination of the easement, if desired, would seem appropriate. Even with an offer of partial subordination, institutional resistance by lenders to financing easement-burdened properties—driven in part, reportedly, by secondary market concerns over marketability—will have to be overcome.[48] The following is an example of one way the issue might be addressed.

>**Future Mortgages.** Upon request, Grantee agrees to subordinate its rights under this Easement to the valid claims of any future mortgage holders or beneficiaries of deeds of trust to the proceeds of any sale, condemnation proceedings, or insurance involving the Property, or to the leases, rents, and profits thereof, and likewise to subordinate its rights under any lien that may be created by Grantee's exercise of any of its rights under this Easement after the date of such subordination; provided that any such mortgage or deed of trust shall remain subordinated and junior to the Easement to the extent necessary to permit Grantee to enforce the purpose of this Easement in perpetuity and to prevent any modification or extinguishment of this Easement by the exercise of any rights of such mortgage holder or trust deed beneficiary; and provided further that, in the unlikely event this Easement is terminated under the circumstances described in section 9, Grantee shall be entitled to compensation in accordance with the terms of section 9. Grantee agrees to execute any documents required to effect a subordination pursuant to this paragraph.

Under some circumstances, as even the IRS regulations acknowledge, subordination of an existing mortgage or deed of trust may prove unnecessary. *See* Treas. Reg. § 1.170A-14(g)(2). Nevertheless, the parties should review the financing documents and, if necessary, consult with the lender or legal counsel to determine whether creation of the easement might trigger any due-on-sale or due-on-encumbrance clause in the mortgage or deed of trust. If so, a waiver or consent agreement should be sought from the mortgage holder.

---

48. *See* Andrew Bowman, *Conservation Easement Properties as Collateral: The Need to Ensure Access to Mortgage Financing*, The Back Forty, January/February 1994, at 1.

2 Model Historic Preservation Easement and Commentary

Model Historic Preservation Easement and Commentary

Stefan Nagel

Introduction

The model historic preservation easement is loosely based on the preservation easement edited and adapted by this author for the 1987 edition of *The Conservation Easement Handbook* from drafts prepared by Richard J. Roddewig and Cheryl A. Inghram, currently of Clarion Associates, Chicago, Illinois. The author has, however, substantially refined and modified the model easement to comport with developments in easement transaction practice, real estate law generally, and tax law specifically.

The commentary that follows the model historic preservation easement is intended to supplement the commentary to the revised model conservation easement. Consequently, the analysis, tax and legal references, recommendations and admonitions of the latter commentary should be reviewed as well to gain a better understanding of the underlying legal and practical considerations that form the conceptual basis for the model historic preservation easement.

An important note on nomenclature: Although the easement is designated as a "model" easement, *no one easement document can be used universally in every potential easement donation situation*. The variables of state law, the characteristics of the property intended to be protected, donor intentions, donee expectations, and the fact that the Internal Revenue Service has never approved a "safe harbor" document mean that no one document truly can be considered a model. The terms of the model easement may and should be modified to address these variables as long as those provisions required under the easement regulations and state law are adequately addressed.

The model historic preservation easement has been prepared to meet a particular set of circumstances: a historically or architecturally significant residence, including ancillary structures, on a fairly large site. In such a situation, the relationship between the buildings and their setting is as important as the structures themselves. The terms "the Residence" and "Ancillary Structures," and the setting in which they are located, have been carefully defined for purposes of this model and the assumed set of circumstances. In a different context in which, for example, there may be only one building on the property, or only the facades are protected, the easement may be accordingly simplified.

Checklists

Checklist I
Model Historic Preservation Easement
Complete Outline

CAPTION (Parties and Date)

RECITALS

- Property Description
- Contributing Features
- Authorizing State Law
- Qualifications of Grantee
- Affirmative Recitals of Historic Certification or Significance
- Mutual Recognition of Significance
- Baseline Documentation
- Mutual Statements of Intent to Grant and Accept

GRANT (Perpetuity)

PURPOSE

    1.   Purpose

GRANTOR'S COVENANTS

    2.1 Covenant to Maintain
    2.2 Prohibited Activities

GRANTOR'S CONDITIONAL RIGHTS

    3.1 Conditional Rights Requiring Approval of Grantee
    3.2 Review of Grantor's Requests for Approval
    4.   Standards for Review
    5.   Public Access

GRANTOR'S RESERVED RIGHTS

    6.   Grantor's Reserved Rights Not Requiring Further Approval by Grantee

CASUALTY DAMAGE OR DESTRUCTION; INSURANCE

    7.   Casualty Damage or Destruction
    8.   Review After Casualty Damage or Destruction
    9.   Insurance

INDEMNIFICATION; TAXES

    10. Indemnification
    11. Taxes

ADMINISTRATION AND ENFORCEMENT

    12.   Written Notice
    13.   Evidence of Compliance
    14.   Inspection
    15.   Grantee's Remedies
    16.   Notice from Government Authorities
    17.   Notice of Proposed Sale
    18.   Liens
    19.   Plaque

BINDING EFFECT; ASSIGNMENT

    20.   Runs with the Land
    21.   Assignment
    22.   Recording and Effective Date

PERCENTAGE INTERESTS; EXTINGUISHMENT

    23.1   Percentage Interests
    23.2   Extinguishment
    23.3   Condemnation

INTERPRETATION

    24.   Interpretation

AMENDMENT

    25.   Amendment

MORTGAGE SUBORDINATION

    26.   Mortgage Subordination (Supplementary Provision)

HABENDUM

SIGNATURES AND ACKNOWLEDGMENTS

EXHIBITS

    A.   Property Description

Checklist II
Provisions Relating to IRS Requirements
(Treas. Reg. § 1.170A-14)

RECITALS

- Contributing Features
- Qualifications of Grantee
- Affirmative Recitals of Historic Certification or Significance
- Baseline Documentation

GRANT (Perpetuity)

PROVISIONS

1.	Purpose
2.1	Covenant to Maintain
2.2	Prohibited Activities
3.1	Conditional Rights Requiring Approval of Grantee
4.	Standards for Review
5.	Public Access
14.	Inspection
15.	Grantee's Remedies
20.	Runs with the Land
21.	Assignment
22.	Recording and Effective Date
23.1	Percentage Interests
23.2	Extinguishment
23.3	Condemnation
25.	Mortgage Subordination (if property encumbered with preexisting mortgage or deed of trust)

Model Historic Preservation Easement

Note: The boxed numbers inserted in the text of the easement correspond with the subheading numbers in the commentary that follows. Optional provisions inserted in brackets are discussed in the commentary.

THIS PRESERVATION AND CONSERVATION EASEMENT DEED, made this _____ day of ____[month]____, _[year]_, by and between _____ ("Grantor") and _____ ("Grantee"), a nonprofit corporation of [state of incorporation].

WITNESSETH:

WHEREAS, Grantor is owner in fee simple of certain real property located in the Town of _____, _____ County, [state], more particularly described in Exhibit A attached hereto and incorporated herein (hereinafter "the Property"), said Property including the following structures (hereinafter "the Buildings"): [1] [2]

the principal residence constructed of ____[brief description]____ dating from [year] (hereinafter "the Residence"); and additional ancillary structures [describe] (hereinafter "the Ancillary Structures").

[WHEREAS, the Property also includes a formal landscaped garden, [describe]___, designed by noted landscape architect ____[name]____ (hereinafter "the Garden");]

WHEREAS, the Property has significant undeveloped open space, including fields, forests, and [describe other], that contributes to the setting, context, and the public's view of the Buildings;

WHEREAS, Grantee is authorized to accept preservation and conservation easements to protect property significant in national and [state] history and culture under the provisions of [state easement legislation] (hereinafter "the Act");

WHEREAS, Grantee is a publicly supported, tax-exempt, nonprofit organization whose primary purposes include the preservation and conservation of sites, buildings, and objects of national significance and is a qualifying recipient of qualified conservation contributions under Section 170(h) of the Internal Revenue Code of 1986, as amended, and the regulations thereunder (hereinafter, "the Code");

WHEREAS, the Property stands as a significant example of _____ style architecture in [state], illustrates aesthetics of design and setting, and possesses integrity of materials and workmanship;

WHEREAS, because of its architectural, historic, and cultural significance the Property was listed in the National Register of Historic Places on [date] and is a certified historic structure [or historically important land area] under Section 170(h)(4)(B) of the Code;

WHEREAS, Grantor and Grantee recognize the architectural, historic, and cultural values (hereinafter "conservation and preservation values") and significance of the Property, and have the common purpose of conserving and preserving the aforesaid conservation and preservation values and significance of the Property;

WHEREAS, the Property's conservation and preservation values are documented in a set of reports, drawings, and photographs (hereinafter, "Baseline Documentation") incorporated herein by reference, which Baseline Documentation the parties agree provides an accurate representation of the Property as of the effective date of this grant. In the event of any discrepancy between the two counterparts produced, the counterpart retained by Grantee shall control; [3]

WHEREAS, the Baseline Documentation shall consist of the following: _____[list documents and materials]_____;

WHEREAS, the grant of a preservation and conservation easement by Grantor to Grantee on the Property will assist in preserving and maintaining the Property and its architectural, historic, and cultural features for the benefit of the people of the Town [County] of _____, the State of _____, and the United States of America;

WHEREAS, to that end, Grantor desires to grant to Grantee, and Grantee desires to accept, a preservation and conservation easement (hereinafter, the "Easement") in gross in perpetuity on the Property pursuant to the Act.

NOW, THEREFORE, in consideration of Ten Dollars ($10.00) and other good and valuable consideration, receipt of which is hereby acknowledged, and pursuant to Section 170(h) of the Code and [give full citation to the state easement legislation] Grantor does hereby voluntarily grant and convey unto the Grantee a preservation and conservation easement in gross in perpetuity over the Property described in Exhibit A.

PURPOSE [4]

1. **Purpose.** It is the Purpose of this Easement to assure that the architectural, historic, cultural, and associated open space features of the Property will be retained and maintained forever substantially in their current condition for conservation and preservation purposes and to prevent any use or change of the Property that will significantly impair or interfere with the Property's conservation and preservation values.

GRANTOR'S COVENANTS [5]

2.1 **Grantor's Covenants: Covenant to Maintain.** Grantor agrees at all times to maintain the Buildings in the same structural condition and state of repair to that existing on the effective date of this Easement. Grantor's obligation to maintain shall require replacement, repair, and reconstruction by Grantor whenever necessary to preserve the Buildings in substantially the same structural condition and state of repair as that existing on the date of this Easement. Grantor's obligation to maintain shall also require that the Property's landscaping be maintained in good appearance with substantially similar plantings, vegetation, and natural screening to that existing on the effective date of this Easement. The existing lawn areas shall be maintained as lawns, regularly mown. The existing meadows and open fields shall be maintained as meadows and open fields, regularly bushhogged to prevent the growth of woody vegetation where none currently grows. Subject to the casualty provisions of paragraphs 7 and 8, this obligation to maintain shall require replacement, rebuilding, repair, and reconstruction of the Buildings whenever necessary in accordance with *The Secretary of the Interior's Standards for Rehabilitation and Guidelines for Rehabilitating Historic Buildings* (36 C.F.R. § 67), as these may be amended from time to time (hereinafter the "Secretary's Standards").

2.2 **Grantor's Covenants: Prohibited Activities**. The following acts or uses are expressly forbidden on, over, or under the Property, except as otherwise conditioned in this paragraph:

(a) the Buildings shall not be demolished, removed, or razed except as provided in paragraphs 7 and 8;

(b) nothing shall be erected or allowed to grow on the Property which would impair the visibility of the Property and the Buildings from street level;

(c) no other buildings or structures, including satellite receiving dishes (small rooftop dishes excluded), camping accommodations, or mobile homes, shall be erected or placed on the Property hereafter except for temporary structures required for the maintenance or rehabilitation of the Property, such as construction trailers;

(d) the dumping of ashes, trash, rubbish, or any other unsightly or offensive materials is prohibited on the Property;

(e) the Property shall not be divided or subdivided in law or in fact and the Property shall not be devised or conveyed except as a unit;

(f) no above-ground utility transmission lines, except those reasonably necessary for the existing Buildings, may be created on the Property, subject to utility easements already recorded;

(g) subject to the maintenance covenants of paragraph 2.1 hereof, the following features located within the Residence [or Buildings/Ancillary Structures] shall not be removed, demolished, or altered:

[Specific interior features that are to be protected are described here]

GRANTOR'S CONDITIONAL RIGHTS [6]

3.1 Conditional Rights Requiring Approval by Grantee. Without the prior express written approval of the Grantee, which approval may be withheld or conditioned in the sole discretion of Grantee, Grantor shall not undertake any of the following actions:

(a) increase or decrease the height of, make additions to, change the exterior construction materials or colors of, or move, improve, alter, reconstruct, or change the facades (including fenestration) and roofs of the Buildings;

(b) change the floor plan of the Residence [or Buildings/Ancillary Structures];

(c) erect any external signs or external advertisements except: (i) such plaque permitted under paragraph 19 of this easement; (ii) a sign stating solely the address of the Property; and (iii) a temporary sign to advertise the sale or rental of the Property;

(d) make permanent substantial topographical changes, such as, by example, excavation for the construction of roads and recreational facilities;

(e) cut down or otherwise remove live trees located within existing lawn areas, or cut down or otherwise remove live trees located outside the existing lawn areas, meadows and open fields for the purpose of conducting commercial timber production [or allow conditional harvesting of timber in accordance with qualified plan presented to Grantee for approval. *(See Model Conservation Easement)*]; and

(f) change the use of the Property to another use other than single family residential. Grantee must determine that the proposed use: (i) does not impair the significant conservation and preservation values of the Property; and (ii) does not conflict with the Purpose of the Easement.

3.2 **Review of Grantor's Requests for Approval**. Grantor shall submit to Grantee for Grantee's approval of those conditional rights set out at paragraph 3.1 two copies of information (including plans, specifications, and designs where appropriate) identifying the proposed activity with reasonable specificity. In connection therewith, Grantor shall also submit to Grantee a timetable for the proposed activity sufficient to permit Grantee to monitor such activity. Within 45 (forty-five) days of Grantee's receipt of any plan or written request for approval hereunder, Grantee shall certify in writing that (a) it approves the plan or request, or (b) it disapproves the plan or request as submitted, in which case Grantee shall provide Grantor with written suggestions for modification or a written explanation for Grantee's disapproval. Any failure by Grantee to act within 45 (forty-five) days of receipt of Grantor's submission or resubmission of plans or requests shall be deemed to constitute approval by Grantee of the plan or request as submitted and to permit Grantor to undertake the proposed activity in accordance with the plan or request submitted.

4. **Standards for Review**. In exercising any authority created by the Easement to inspect the Property or the interior of the Residence; to review any construction, alteration, repair, or maintenance; or to review casualty damage or to reconstruct or approve reconstruction of the Building following casualty damage, Grantee shall apply the Secretary's Standards.

5. **Public Access**. Grantor shall make the Property and interior of the Residence accessible to the public on a minimum of _____ days per year. At other times deemed reasonable by Grantor persons affiliated with educational organizations, professional architectural associations, and historical societies shall be admitted to study the property. Grantee may make photographs, drawings, or other representations documenting the significant historical, cultural, and architectural character and features of the property and distribute them to magazines, newsletters, or other publicly available publications, or use them to fulfill its charitable and educational purposes. [7]

GRANTOR'S RESERVED RIGHTS [8]

6. Grantor's Reserved Rights Not Requiring Further Approval by Grantee. Subject to the provisions of paragraphs 2.1, 2.2, and 3.1, the following rights, uses, and activities of or by Grantor on, over, or under the Property are permitted by this Easement and by Grantee without further approval by Grantee:

(a) the right to engage in all those acts and uses that: (i) are permitted by governmental statute or regulation; (ii) do not substantially impair the conservation and preservation values of the Property; and (iii) are not inconsistent with the Purpose of this Easement;

(b) pursuant to the provisions of paragraph 2.1, the right to maintain and repair the Buildings strictly according to the Secretary's Standards. As used in this subparagraph, the right to maintain and repair shall mean the use by Grantor of in-kind materials and colors, applied with workmanship comparable to that which was used in the construction or application of those materials being repaired or maintained, for the purpose of retaining in good condition the appearance and construction of the Buildings. The right to maintain and repair as used in this subparagraph shall not include the right to make changes in appearance, materials, colors, and workmanship from that existing prior to the maintenance and repair without the prior approval of Grantee in accordance with the provisions of paragraphs 3.1 and 3.2;

(c) the right to continue all manner of existing residential use and enjoyment of the Property's Buildings and Garden, including but not limited to the maintenance, repair, and restoration of existing fences; the right to maintain existing driveways, roads, and paths with the use of same or similar surface materials; the right to maintain existing utility lines, gardening and building walkways, steps, and garden fences; the right to cut, remove, and clear grass or other vegetation and to perform routine maintenance, landscaping, horticultural activities, and upkeep, consistent with the Purpose of this Easement; and

(d) the right to conduct at or on the Property educational and nonprofit activities that are not inconsistent with the protection of the conservation and preservation values of the Property.

CASUALTY DAMAGE OR DESTRUCTION; INSURANCE [9]

7. Casualty Damage or Destruction. In the event that the Buildings or any part thereof shall be damaged or destroyed by fire, flood, windstorm, hurricane, earth movement, or other casualty, Grantor shall notify Grantee in writing within fourteen (14) days of the damage or destruction, such notification including what, if any, emergency work has already been completed. No repairs or reconstruction of any type, other than temporary emergency work to prevent further damage to the Buildings and to protect public safety, shall be undertaken by Grantor without Grantee's prior written approval. Within thirty (30) days of the date of damage or destruction, if required by Grantee, Grantor at its expense shall submit to the Grantee a written report prepared by a qualified restoration architect and an engineer who are acceptable to Grantor and

Grantee, which report shall include the following:

    (a) an assessment of the nature and extent of the damage;

    (b) a determination of the feasibility of the restoration of the Buildings and/or reconstruction of damaged or destroyed portions of the Buildings; and

    (c) a report of such restoration/reconstruction work necessary to return the Buildings to the condition existing at the date hereof.

8. **Review After Casualty Damage or Destruction**. If, after reviewing the report provided in paragraph 7 and assessing the availability of insurance proceeds after satisfaction of any mortgagee's/lender's claims under paragraph 9, Grantor and Grantee agree that the Purpose of the Easement will be served by such restoration/reconstruction, Grantor and Grantee shall establish a schedule under which Grantor shall complete the restoration/reconstruction of the Buildings in accordance with plans and specifications consented to by the parties up to at least the total of the casualty insurance proceeds available to Grantor.

If, after reviewing the report and assessing the availability of insurance proceeds after satisfaction of any mortgagee's/lender's claims under paragraph 9, Grantor and Grantee agree that restoration/reconstruction of the Property is impractical or impossible, or agree that the Purpose of the Easement would not be served by such restoration/reconstruction, Grantor may, with the prior written consent of Grantee, alter, demolish, remove, or raze one or more of the Buildings, and/or construct new improvements on the Property. Grantor and Grantee may agree to extinguish this Easement in whole or in part in accordance with the laws of the State of _____ and paragraph 23.2 hereof.

If, after reviewing the report and assessing the availability of insurance proceeds after satisfaction of any mortgagee's/lender's claims under paragraph 9, Grantor and Grantee are unable to agree that the Purpose of the Easement will or will not be served by such restoration/reconstruction, the matter may be referred by either party to binding arbitration and settled in accordance with the State of _____ arbitration statute then in effect [or refer to the arbitration provision referenced at paragraph 15, below].

9. **Insurance**. Grantor shall keep the Property insured by an insurance company rated "A1" or better by Best's for the full replacement value against loss from the perils commonly insured under standard fire and extended coverage policies and comprehensive general liability insurance against claims for personal injury, death, and property damage. Property damage insurance shall include change in condition and building ordinance coverage, in form and amount sufficient to replace fully the damaged Property and Buildings without cost or expense to Grantor or contribution or coinsurance from Grantor. Such insurance shall include Grantee's interest and name Grantee as an additional insured. Grantor shall deliver to Grantee, within ten (10) business days of Grantee's written request therefor, certificates of such insurance coverage. Provided, however, that whenever the Property is encumbered with a mortgage or deed of trust, nothing contained in this paragraph shall jeopardize the prior claim, if any, of the mortgagee/lender to the insurance proceeds.

INDEMNIFICATION; TAXES [10]

10. **Indemnification**. Grantor hereby agrees to pay, protect, indemnify, hold harmless and defend at its own cost and expense, Grantee, its agents, directors and employees, or independent contractors from and against any and all claims, liabilities, expenses, costs, damages, losses, and expenditures (including reasonable attorneys' fees and disbursements hereafter incurred) arising out of or in connection with injury to or death of any person; physical damage to the Property; the presence or release in, on, or about the Property, at any time, of any substance now or hereafter defined, listed, or otherwise classified pursuant to any law, ordinance, or regulation as a hazardous, toxic, polluting, or contaminating substance; or other injury or other damage occurring on or about the Property, unless such injury or damage is caused by Grantee or any agent, trustee, employee, or contractor of Grantee. In the event that Grantor is required to indemnify Grantee pursuant to the terms of this paragraph, the amount of such indemnity, until discharged, shall constitute a lien on the Property with the same effect and priority as a mechanic's lien. Provided, however, that nothing contained herein shall jeopardize the priority of any recorded lien of mortgage or deed of trust given in connection with a promissory note secured by the Property.

11. **Taxes**. Grantor shall pay immediately, when first due and owing, all general taxes, special taxes, special assessments, water charges, sewer service charges, and other charges which may become a lien on the Property unless Grantor timely objects to the amount or validity of the assessment or charge and diligently prosecutes an appeal thereof, in which case the obligation hereunder to pay such charges shall be suspended for the period permitted by law for prosecuting such appeal and any applicable grace period following completion of such action. In place of Grantor, Grantee is hereby authorized, but in no event required or expected, to make or advance upon three (3) days prior written notice to Grantor any payment relating to taxes, assessments, water rates, sewer rentals and other governmental or municipality charge, fine, imposition, or lien asserted against the Property. Grantee may make such payment according to any bill, statement, or estimate procured from the appropriate public office without inquiry into the accuracy of such bill, statement, or assessment or into the validity of such tax, assessment, sale, or forfeiture. Such payment if made by Grantee shall constitute a lien on the Property with the same effect and priority as a mechanic's lien, except that such lien shall not jeopardize the priority of any recorded lien of mortgage or deed of trust given in connection with a promissory note secured by the Property.

ADMINISTRATION AND ENFORCEMENT

12. **Written Notice**. Any notice which either Grantor or Grantee may desire or be required to give to the other party shall be in writing and shall be delivered by one of the following methods—by overnight courier postage prepaid, facsimile transmission, registered or certified mail with return receipt requested, or hand delivery; if to Grantor, then at _____[address]_____, and if to Grantee, then to _____[address]_____.

Each party may change its address set forth herein by a notice to such effect to the other party. [11]

13. **Evidence of Compliance**. Upon request by Grantee, Grantor shall promptly furnish Grantee with certification that, to the best of Grantee's knowledge, Grantor is in compliance with the obligations of Grantor contained herein, or that otherwise evidences the status of this Easement to the extent of Grantee's knowledge thereof. [12]

14. **Inspection**. With the consent of Grantor, representatives of Grantee shall be permitted at all reasonable times to inspect the Property, including the interior of the Residence [or Buildings/Ancillary Structures]. Grantor covenants not to withhold unreasonably its consent in determining dates and times for such inspections. [13]

15. **Grantee's Remedies**. Grantee may, following reasonable written notice to Grantor, institute suit(s) to enjoin any violation of the terms of this easement by *ex parte*, temporary, preliminary, and/or permanent injunction, including prohibitory and/or mandatory injunctive relief, and to require the restoration of the Property and Buildings to the condition and appearance that existed prior to the violation complained of. Grantee shall also have available all legal and other equitable remedies to enforce Grantor's obligations hereunder.

[Supplementary arbitration provision may be added here or elsewhere. (*See model conservation easement.*)]

In the event Grantor is found to have violated any of its obligations, Grantor shall reimburse Grantee for any costs or expenses incurred in connection with Grantee's enforcement of the terms of this Easement, including all reasonable court costs, and attorney's, architectural, engineering, and expert witness fees.

Exercise by Grantee of one remedy hereunder shall not have the effect of waiving or limiting any other remedy, and the failure to exercise any remedy shall not have the effect of waiving or limiting the use of any other remedy or the use of such remedy at any other time. [14]

16. **Notice from Government Authorities**. Grantor shall deliver to Grantee copies of any notice of violation or lien relating to the Property received by Grantor from any government authority within five (5) days of receipt by Grantor. Upon request by Grantee, Grantor shall promptly furnish Grantee with evidence of Grantor's compliance with such notice or lien where compliance is required by law. [15]

17. **Notice of Proposed Sale**. Grantor shall promptly notify Grantee in writing of any proposed sale of the Property and provide the opportunity for Grantee to explain the terms of the Easement to potential new owners prior to sale closing.

18. **Liens**. Any lien on the Property created pursuant to any paragraph of this Easement may be confirmed by judgment and foreclosed by Grantee in the same manner as a mechanic's lien, except that no lien created pursuant to this

Easement shall jeopardize the priority of any recorded lien of mortgage or deed of trust given in connection with a promissory note secured by the Property. [16]

19. **Plaque**. Grantor agrees that Grantee may provide and maintain a plaque on the Property, which plaque shall not exceed 24 by 24 inches in size, giving notice of the significance of the Property and the existence of this Easement. [17]

BINDING EFFECT; ASSIGNMENT

20. **Runs with the Land**. Except as provided in paragraphs 8 and 23.2, the obligations imposed by this Easement shall be effective in perpetuity and shall be deemed to run as a binding servitude with the Property. This Easement shall extend to and be binding upon Grantor and Grantee, their respective successors in interest and all persons hereafter claiming under or through Grantor and Grantee, and the words "Grantor" and "Grantee" when used herein shall include all such persons. Any right, title, or interest herein granted to Grantee also shall be deemed granted to each successor and assign of Grantee and each such following successor and assign thereof, and the word "Grantee" shall include all such successors and assigns.

Anything contained herein to the contrary notwithstanding, an owner of the Property shall have no obligation pursuant to this instrument where such owner shall cease to have any ownership interest in the Property by reason of a *bona fide* transfer. The restrictions, stipulations, and covenants contained in this Easement shall be inserted by Grantor, verbatim or by express reference, in any subsequent deed or other legal instrument by which Grantor divests itself of either the fee simple title to or any lesser estate in the Property or any part thereof, including by way of example and not limitation, a lease of all or a portion of the Property. [18]

21. **Assignment**. Grantee may convey, assign, or transfer this Easement to a unit of federal, state, or local government or to a similar local, state, or national organization that is a "qualified organization" under Section 170(h) of the Code whose purposes, *inter alia*, are to promote preservation or conservation of historical, cultural, or architectural resources, provided that any such conveyance, assignment, or transfer requires that the Purpose for which the Easement was granted will continue to be carried out. [19]

22. **Recording and Effective Date**. Grantee shall do and perform at its own cost all acts necessary to the prompt recording of this instrument in the land records of [town, county, or regional district], [state]. Grantor and Grantee intend that the restrictions arising under this Easement take effect on the day and year this instrument is recorded in the land records of [town, county, or regional district], [state]. [20]

PERCENTAGE INTERESTS; EXTINGUISHMENT [21]

23.1 **Percentage Interests**. For purposes of allocating proceeds pursuant to paragraphs 23.2 and 23.3, Grantor and Grantee stipulate that as of the date of this Easement, Grantor and Grantee are each vested with real property interests in the Property and that such interests have a stipulated percentage interest in the fair market value of the Property. Said percentage interests shall be determined by the ratio of the value of the Easement on the effective date of this Easement to the value of the Property, without deduction for the value of the Easement, on the effective date of this Easement. The values on the effective date of the Easement shall be those values used to calculate the deduction for federal income tax purposes allowable by reason of this grant, pursuant to Section 170(h) of the Code. The parties shall include the ratio of those values with the Baseline Documentation (on file with Grantor and Grantee) and shall amend such values, if necessary, to reflect any final determination thereof by the Internal Revenue Service or court of competent jurisdiction. For purposes of this paragraph, the ratio of the value of the Easement to the value of the Property unencumbered by the Easement shall remain constant, and the percentage interests of Grantor and Grantee in the fair market value of the Property thereby determinable shall remain constant, except that the value of any improvements made by Grantor after the effective date of this Easement is reserved to Grantor.

23.2 **Extinguishment**. Grantor and Grantee hereby recognize that circumstances may arise that may make impossible the continued ownership or use of the Property in a manner consistent with the Purpose of this Easement and necessitate extinguishment of the Easement. Such circumstances may include, but are not limited to, partial or total destruction of the Buildings resulting from casualty. Extinguishment must be the result of a judicial proceeding in a court of competent jurisdiction. Unless otherwise required by applicable law at the time, in the event of any sale of all or a portion of the Property (or any other property received in connection with an exchange or involuntary conversion of the Property) after such termination or extinguishment, and after the satisfaction of prior claims and any costs or expenses associated with such sale, Grantor and Grantee shall share in any net proceeds resulting from such sale in accordance with their respective percentage interests in the fair market value of the Property, as such interests are determined under the provisions of paragraph 23.1, adjusted, if necessary, to reflect a partial termination or extinguishment of this Easement. All such proceeds received by Grantee shall be used by Grantee in a manner consistent with Grantee's primary purposes. Net proceeds shall also include, without limitation, net insurance proceeds.

In the event of extinguishment, the provisions of this paragraph shall survive extinguishment and shall constitute a lien on the Property with the same effect and priority as a mechanic's lien, except that such lien shall not jeopardize the priority of any recorded lien of mortgage or deed of trust given in connection with a promissory note secured by the Property.

23.3 **Condemnation**. If all or any part of the Property is taken under the power of eminent domain by public, corporate, or other authority, or otherwise acquired by such authority through a purchase in lieu of a taking, Grantor and Grantee shall join in appropriate proceedings at the time of such taking to recover the full value of those interests in the Property that are subject to the taking and all incidental and direct damages resulting from the taking. After the satisfaction of prior claims and net of expenses reasonably incurred by Grantor and Grantee in connection with such taking, Grantor and Grantee shall be respectively entitled to compensation from the balance of the recovered proceeds in conformity with the provisions of paragraphs 23.1 and 23.2 unless otherwise provided by law.

INTERPRETATION [22]

24. **Interpretation.** The following provisions shall govern the effectiveness, interpretation, and duration of the Easement.

(a) Any rule of strict construction designed to limit the breadth of restrictions on alienation or use of Property shall not apply in the construction or interpretation of this Easement, and this instrument shall be interpreted broadly to effect its Purpose and the transfer of rights and the restrictions on use herein contained.

(b) This instrument may be executed in two counterparts, one of which may be retained by Grantor and the other, after recording, to be retained by Grantee. In the event of any disparity between the counterparts produced, the recorded counterpart shall in all cases govern.

(c) This instrument is made pursuant to the Act, but the invalidity of such Act or any part thereof shall not affect the validity and enforceability of this Easement according to its terms, it being the intent of the parties to agree and to bind themselves, their successors, and their assigns in perpetuity to each term of this instrument whether this instrument be enforceable by reason of any statute, common law, or private agreement in existence either now or hereafter. The invalidity or unenforceability of any provision of this instrument shall not affect the validity or enforceability of any other provision of this instrument or any ancillary or supplementary agreement relating to the subject matter thereof.

(d) Nothing contained herein shall be interpreted to authorize or permit Grantor to violate any ordinance or regulation relating to building materials, construction methods, or use. In the event of any conflict between any such ordinance or regulation and the terms hereof, Grantor promptly shall notify Grantee of such conflict and shall cooperate with Grantee and the applicable governmental entity to accommodate the purposes of both this Easement and such ordinance or regulation.

(e) To the extent that Grantor owns or is entitled to development rights which may exist now or at some time hereafter by reason of the fact that under any applicable zoning or similar ordinance the Property may be developed to use more intensive (in terms of height, bulk, or other objective criteria related by such ordinances) than the Property is devoted as of the date hereof, such development rights shall not be exercisable on, above, or below the Property during the term of the Easement, nor shall they be transferred to any adjacent parcel and exercised in a manner that would interfere with the Purpose of the Easement.

AMENDMENT [23]

25. **Amendment**. If circumstances arise under which an amendment to or modification of this Easement would be appropriate, Grantor and Grantee may by mutual written agreement jointly amend this Easement, provided that no amendment shall be made that will adversely affect the qualification of this Easement or the status of Grantee under any applicable laws, including Sections 170(h) and 501(c)(3) of the Code and the laws of the State of _____. Any such amendment shall be consistent with the protection of the conservation and preservation values of the Property and the Purpose of this Easement; shall not affect its perpetual duration; shall not permit additional residential development on the Property other than the residential development permitted by this Easement on its effective date; shall not permit any private inurement to any person or entity; and shall not adversely impact the overall architectural, historic, natural habitat, and open space values protected by this Easement. Any such amendment shall be recorded in the land records of [town, county, or regional district], [state]. Nothing in this paragraph shall require Grantor or Grantee to agree to any amendment or to consult or negotiate regarding any amendment.

THIS EASEMENT reflects the entire agreement of Grantor and Grantee. Any prior or simultaneous correspondence, understandings, agreements, and representations are null and void upon execution hereof, unless set out in this instrument.

TO HAVE AND TO HOLD, the said Preservation and Conservation Easement, unto the said Grantee and its successors and permitted assigns forever. This DEED OF PRESERVATION AND CONSERVATION EASEMENT may be executed in two counterparts and by each party on a separate counterpart, each of which when so executed and delivered shall be an original, but both of which together shall constitute one instrument.

IN WITNESS WHEREOF, Grantor and Grantee have set their hands under seal on the days and year set forth below.

WITNESS: GRANTOR:

_____   _____

_____   _____
                                                                  (date)

ATTEST: GRANTEE:

By: _____   By: _____
                                           Its President   (date)

[Notarization]

SCHEDULE OF EXHIBITS

A. Property Description

Supplementary Mortgage Subordination paragraph to follow paragraph 25:

MORTGAGE SUBORDINATION [24]

26. At the time of the conveyance of this Easement, the Property is subject to a Mortgage/Deed of Trust dated _____, recorded on _____, in the _____ Land Records at Book/Liber _____ Page/Folio _____ (hereinafter "the Mortgage"/"the Deed of Trust") held by _____ (hereinafter, "Mortgagee"/"Lender"). The Mortgagee/Lender joins in the execution of this Easement to evidence its agreement to subordinate the Mortgage/the Deed of Trust to this Easement under the following conditions and stipulations:

(a) The Mortgagee/Lender and its assignees shall have a prior claim to all insurance proceeds as a result of any casualty, hazard, or accident occurring to or about the Property and all proceeds of condemnation proceedings, and shall be entitled to same in preference to Grantee until the Mortgage/the Deed of Trust is paid off and discharged, notwithstanding that the Mortgage/the Deed of Trust is subordinate in priority to the Easement.

(b) If the Mortgagee/Lender receives an assignment of the leases, rents, and profits of the Property as security or additional security for the loan secured by the Mortgage/Deed of Trust, then the Mortgagee/Lender shall have a prior claim to the leases, rents, and profits of the Property and shall be entitled to receive same in preference to Grantee until the Mortgagee's/Lender's debt is paid off or otherwise satisfied, notwithstanding that the Mortgage/Deed of Trust is subordinate in priority to the Easement.

(c) The Mortgagee/Lender or purchaser in foreclosure shall have no obligation, debt, or liability under the Easement until the Mortgagee/Lender or a purchaser in foreclosure under it obtains ownership of the Property. In the event of foreclosure or deed in lieu of foreclosure, the Easement is not extinguished.

(d) Nothing contained in this paragraph or in this Easement shall be construed to give any Mortgagee/Lender the right to violate the terms of this Easement or to extinguish this Easement by taking title to the Property by foreclosure or otherwise.

Commentary

Note: The numbers at the beginnings of the subheads in this section correspond with the boxed numbers inserted in the text of the model historic preservation easement preceding this commentary. Reference to the appropriate numbered paragraphs in the model appears in parentheses.

1. Recitals (The "Whereas" Clauses)

In accordance with standard real estate transaction practice and requirements of state real estate law, the model document opens with the naming of the grantor and grantee. The names of the record owner of the property making the donation and the easement grantee need to be provided in each transaction.

State real estate law and practice dictate what additional information needs to be included, such as the form of the document, signature lines, acknowledgment language, use of addresses, legal standing, and state of incorporation. Note that most, but not all, states have enacted some form of easement-enabling legislation. While many of these statutes are based on the Uniform Conservation Easement Act, many are not. It is therefore essential that an attorney experienced in state transactional requirements participate in the drafting or review of every easement.

A series of introductory recitals, each beginning with "whereas," sets out the legal basis for the donation under state enabling and federal tax law, and gives some information about the historic and architectural significance of the property. If the property is listed in the National Register of Historic Places, or is a contributing property in a National Register district, or may otherwise be deemed a "historically important land area" under Section 170(h)(4)(B) of the Internal Revenue Code (hereinafter, "the Code"), that fact should be mentioned.

It is important to include a few pertinent facts from the National Register nomination or from other documentation that explain the historic significance of the property. While this material will be detailed in the baseline documentation, it is equally important to have the significance summarized in what is in effect a public document. This facilitates monitoring and administration of the easement and assures compliance with easement regulation requirements.

2. Legal Description

A precise legal description of each property on which a donation is made needs to be included in the easement document. This may be obtained from a survey, a title report, or other documentation provided by the owner of the property.

3. Baseline Documentation

The Treasury Regulations, at Section 1.170A-14(g)(5)(i) require that the easement donor provide documentation describing the character and condition of the property as of the date of the donation where the donor retains certain rights that may impact the preservation purposes of the donation. The documentation may include photographs, site plans, and other descriptive materials. Typically, counterparts of this documentation, known as "Baseline Documentation," will be kept by the donor and at the offices of the donee for monitoring and enforcement purposes. This record becomes a permanent reference against which all future changes to the property can be measured.

If other portions of the property are to be protected—for example, important natural features—these too should be documented and included in the documentation. The same is true if any interior features are to be protected.

If the property is one proposed for rehabilitation (or is actually undergoing rehabilitation), rehabilitation plans should be included in the baseline documentation. The easement text should require that all work be completed in accordance with the plans, and a deadline for completion specified.

4. Purpose (paragraph 1)

The purpose clause sets out general preservation principles as these relate to the specific property. All requests for approval, possible enforcement actions, and other administrative and legal responses will be measured against the principles set out in the purpose clause. It is therefore important to tailor the purpose clause to those characteristics of the property that make the property historically or architecturally important and to articulate the Grantor's and Grantee's mutual expectations concerning how the property will be used.

5. Grantor's Covenants (paragraph 2)

Paragraph 2.1 of the model document is one of the easement's most important provisions. It carefully sets out the principal maintenance responsibilities and prohibitions imposed upon the current and future owners of the property. While the easement regulations do not generally require that any particular maintenance standard should be used, easement-holding organizations have learned through experience to use and apply The Secretary of the Interior's Standards for Rehabilitation and Guidelines for Rehabilitating Historic Buildings, 36 C.F.R. 67. Even though the Rehabilitation Standards have been superseded to some extent by the more recent Secretary of the Interior's Treatment Standards for Historic Properties (Rev. 1992), easement-holding organizations have gained experience with the older Rehabilitation Standards. Note that easement regulations require that permitted changes to buildings or land areas within a registered historic district may be permitted only if these conform with "appropriate local, state, or Federal standards for construction or rehabilitation within the district." See

Treas. Reg. § 1.170A-14(d)(5)(i). It may therefore be appropriate under certain circumstances to refer to and apply the same design guidelines that have been developed for the historic district.

Actions that are expressly prohibited are set out in paragraph 2.2. To address the requirement of the easement regulations that the public generally be accorded some manner of physical access or ability to view the property, paragraph 2.2(b) requires that the view of the property from street level not be impaired. See Treas. Reg. § 1.170A-14(d)(5)(iv)(A) and also paragraph 5 of the model easement. All other prohibited activities are representative and together assure that no inconsistent use of the property is permitted.

Among the prohibited activities, the prohibition on subdivision may be one of the most contentious in current easement practice. Preservation and conservation organizations are grappling with the issue of whether division of property into multiple ownerships has an impact on the conservation and preservation values of the property or is neutral. Some land trusts are concerned that enforcing subdivision restrictions may be politically difficult. Once permitted, subdivision increases the management burden of enforcing easements on a property that has been fragmented into multiple ownership.

6. Grantor's Conditional Rights (paragraph 3)

No easement document that is intended to be perpetual can anticipate all future uses, alterations, and activities that may be appropriate for a historic property. The property must have some ability to adapt to unforeseeable, perhaps even desirable changed circumstances without impairing preservation principles. The property owner is therefore accorded certain conditional rights that, before they may be exercised, require the approval of the easement-holding organization. Changes in use may be approved by the easement-holding organization provided new uses do not impair significant conservation and preservation values and are not inconsistent with the easement's purpose. See Treas. Reg. § 1.170A-14(e). See also Treas. Reg. § 1.170A-14(g)(5)(d)(ii) requiring prior notification of the easement-holding organization before the property owner may exercise any right which may have an impact on the conservation interests. In the model document, in addition to changes in use, certain exterior and interior alterations are subject to such prior approval. It is important to emphasize that, in reviewing alteration plans, the easement- holding organization will apply the Secretary's Rehabilitation Standards which emphasize repair over replacement, and if replacement is necessary, replacement with like-kind materials over replacement with different materials.

A couple of important caveats: construction of additional floors on a building may affect its architectural integrity and is generally discouraged. Interior work that affects the structural soundness of the building should be reviewed by the easement holder even where the easement doesn't otherwise address interior features.

7. Public Access (paragraph 5)

In addition to the public view provision included at subparagraph 2.2(b), the model easement anticipates that portions of the interior of the protected buildings are under easement protection. If portions of the interior are under easement protection, to assure compliance with the easement regulations, it may be advisable to provide some form of public access to the interior. The easement regulations state:

Where the historic land area or certified historic structure which is the subject of the donation is not visible from a public way (e.g., the structure is hidden from view by a wall or shrubbery, the structure is too far from the public way, or interior characteristics and features of the structure are the subject of the easement), the terms of the easement must be such that the general public is given the opportunity on a regular basis to view the characteristics and features of the property which are preserved by the easement to the extent consistent with the nature and condition of the property. See Treas. Reg. § 1.170A-14(d)(5)(iv)(A).

Among the factors listed in the regulations that determine the type and amount of public access are the following:

- Historical significance of the donated property;

- Nature of the protected features;

- Remoteness or accessibility of the site;

- Possibility of physical hazards to visiting public (e.g., an unoccupied structure in a dilapidated condition);

- Extent to which public access would be an unreasonable intrusion on the owner's privacy;

- Impact of public access upon the preservation interest for which the donation was made;

- Availability of opportunities for public view by means other than site visits.

The regulations provide two examples to illustrate the public access requirements. The first example involves an exterior and interior easement on a house surrounded by a high stone wall which obscures the view from the street. Terms of the easement state that the house may be open to the public from 10 a.m. to 4 p.m. on one Sunday in May and one Sunday in November each year. Tours are to be conducted by the easement-holding organization and visitors must pay a small fee. The easement donee may also photograph the interior and exterior of the house and distribute the photographs. Special appointments may be made by persons affiliated with educational, professional, or historical societies to study the property. At the conclusion of the examples, the regulations include the following statement: "The two opportunities for public visits per year, when combined with the ability of the general public to view the architectural characteristics and features that are the subject of the easement through photographs, the opportunity for scholarly study of the property, and the fact that the house is used as an occupied residence, will enable the donation to satisfy the requirement of public access." See Treas. Reg. § 1.170A-14(d)(5)(v).

The second example involves an unoccupied farmhouse built in the 1840s and located next to a Civil War battlefield. The farmhouse was used during the historic battle, but is not visible from the battlefield or any public road. The battlefield is open to the general public year-round, and the condition of the house is safe for the general public to visit it. The owner of the property donates an easement and provides that the house may be open to the general public on four weekends each year from 8:30 a.m. to 4:00 p.m. According to the regulations, "The donation does not meet the public access requirement because the farmhouse is safe, unoccupied, and easily accessible to the general public who have come to the site to visit Civil War historic land areas (and related resources), but will only be open to the public on four weekends each year." *See* Treas. Reg. § 1.170A-14(d)(5)(v). The Service does conclude that if the farmhouse were open every other weekend during the year, then it might qualify.

8. Grantor's Reserved Rights (paragraph 6)

This paragraph makes clear that any activity or use not regulated or prohibited in the easement is permissible. To protect the conservation and preservation interests on the property (and to qualify for a tax deduction), a number of activities *must be prohibited* (paragraph 2.2). However, some activities that might be destructive of conservation interests can be continued on the property if they are circumscribed and if they are done in a conservation-sensitive manner (paragraphs 3.1 and 6). Note that the "list" in paragraph 6 merely represents a starting point and may be expanded to include other representative rights that do not impair the preservation and conservation values of the property.

9. Casualty Damage or Destruction (paragraphs 7, 8, and 9)

Some of the most important paragraphs in a preservation and conservation easement document concern the rights of each party when the protected property is damaged or destroyed by fire, earthquake, flood, or other casualty. It is also important to understand the relationship between these paragraphs (7 and 8) and the insurance provisions of paragraph 9.

Many preservation easements do not recognize or acknowledge the possibility that casualty damage may justify extinguishment. They merely provide that, in the event of casualty, the terms of the easement will be adapted to the new circumstances. This position may be justified in those cases where the property also consists of extensive fields or other undeveloped land, and continuation of the easement may be appropriate to protect the open space. On the other hand, casualty often renders the property entirely altered. To impose easement covenants on a property whose historic, architectural, or cultural importance has succumbed to casualty merely sets the stage for legal challenge and difficult owner/holder relationships without offsetting preservation benefits. Even in the absence of easement restrictions, properties in historic districts that have undergone casualty will be governed by historic district regulations.

Paragraphs 7 and 8 recognize that properties are destroyed by casualty from time to time. Provision is made to assess the impact of the casualty on the property. If both parties agree that the casualty is of such severity that the purpose of the easement is not served by the property's restoration, the possibility that the easement may be extinguished in accordance with its extinguishment provisions (see paragraph 23.2) is addressed.

In the 1987 model preservation easement, the casualty damage provision included a right of entry and "self-help" provision. The easement holder was authorized to launch a fund campaign to raise the additional cost of the reconstruction and impose this cost as a lien on the property. Or the easement holder was authorized to remove salvageable portions of the facades or other protected features. Those provisions have not been included in this model for three reasons: (1) experience has shown that donors inevitably reject them, (2) many states do not authorize such entry rights, and (3) such entry and "self-help" rights may subject the easement-holding organization to possible liability as an operator under the Comprehensive Environmental Response, Compensation, and Liability Act (CERCLA).

Paragraph 8 requires the property owner to restore or reconstruct damaged structures "up to at least the total of casualty insurance proceeds." This provision implicitly recognizes that casualty insurance is required. Paragraph 9 requires full replacement value insurance with change in condition and building ordinance coverage. In effect, if property is destroyed by casualty, building codes have changed, and the cost of replacement materials at the time of damage has increased beyond current costs of replacement, such insurance is intended to cover these additional, unanticipated expenses. Note that this provision does not require "restoration cost" insurance. An easement-holding organization may wish to require "restoration cost" insurance, but its cost is often prohibitively expensive. Because it is important for easement drafters to understand specific insurance terms, it is helpful while structuring and negotiating insurance provisions to consult with insurance professionals and knowledgable attorneys.

10. Indemnification and Taxes (paragraphs 10 and 11)

Paragraph 10 represents a clear-cut requirement that the owner of the property indemnify and hold the grantee harmless from any and all costs and expenses arising out of or in any way related to injuries to persons, damages to property, and the presence of hazardous wastes. This is intended to provide additional protection to the grantee over and above the requirement that adequate liability and casualty insurance be maintained, naming the grantee as an insured party (see paragraph 9). The indemnification paragraph may be the most important financial protection for the easement holder contained in the model easement.

The reader may also wish to refer to the hazardous waste indemnification provision of the model conservation easement. Issues of hazardous waste are more pronounced in an open space environment. In addition, recent court decisions on hazardous waste liability, while not directly on point, reflect reluctance by the courts to impose liability on non-operators of properties, such as holders of utility easements and owners of other passive, nonpossessory use rights. Therefore, while indemnification from hazardous waste liability is included in the model preservation easement, it is not accorded the same significance or weight as it is in the model conservation easement.

The grantee's ability to pay taxes and assessments that are overdue is a critical right. Where delinquent taxes and assessments are foreclosed by the taxing authorities, the priority of the easement may be jeopardized unless the easement grantee has the authority to protect its position by paying the delinquency. Under the model provision, the grantee's payment may itself constitute a lien against the property, providing additional assurance that the grantee will be reimbursed by the property owner. Because such a lien may take priority over the liens of subordinated or subsequently recorded mortgages or deeds of trust, thereby rendering the property unfinanceable, terms are also included that except current or future mortgages from the grantee's lien.

11. Written Notice (paragraph 12)

Prudently drafted contracts require that notices between parties be in writing to avoid subsequent misunderstanding or even fraud. The addresses to which written notices should be forwarded must be included. The address should include a contact person for the easement-holding organization (identified by position) to avoid the misdirection or misplacement of notices.

12. Evidence of Compliance (paragraph 13)

Subsequent purchasers and lenders will want to know they are not buying into current violations. Compliance certificates are more technically known as "estoppel certificates" which serve to estop, or preclude assertion of a violation by the party certifying that no violations exist.

13. Inspection (paragraph 14)

The easement holder has the right to inspect both the exterior and the interior of the protected property. Reasonable notice of the proposed interior inspection must be given to the property owner, and the owner cannot unreasonably withhold consent in determining dates and times for inspections. The latter provision is significant: in the event of a suspected or imminent violation, it is important that the easement-holding organization have the authority to enter the property.

Interior inspection is an important right that should be provided by every easement document whether or not the easement protects interior as well as exterior features. Such problems as termite infestation, dry rot, flooding or seepage, or foundation settling can eventually threaten not only interior structural integrity but also a protected facade.

14. Grantee's Remedies (paragraph 15)

A variety of legal remedies is provided to the easement grantee to enforce the terms of the model easement. The grantee generally retains all legal and equitable remedies provided in law; some specific authority is itemized as well. Suits to enjoin violation of any term or provision of the easement may be filed, and restoration of the altered or damaged feature to the condition prior to the violation can be sought. See Treas. Reg. § 1.170A-14(g)(5)(ii).

Under the model easement, the easement holder is entitled to be reimbursed for all its legal costs in enforcing the terms of the easement if a court finds that the property owner has violated its terms. These costs include attorney's fees, architectural and engineering fees, and even expert witness fees. There are also other approaches. For example, the parties may agree to pay their own costs, irrespective of the outcome of litigation. The recovery of costs may also be governed by state law.

15. Notice from Government Authorities (paragraph 16)

The property owner must give the grantee written notice, including a copy, of any communication from a government authority about the protected property, and also notice of any proposed sale of the property. The property owner must comply with any demand in a notice from a government authority, and give the grantee an opportunity to explain the terms of the easement to potential new owners of the property.

16. Liens (paragraph 18)

This provision, while redundant, confirms the lien provisions that are provided throughout the document. The right of the grantee to place a lien against the property to guarantee payment of certain expenses incurred by the grantee protects its financial position and is a powerful incentive to the property owner to pay all taxes, judgments, and other charges against the property. Because such grantee's liens may take priority over the liens of subordinated or subsequently recorded mortgages or deeds of trust, thereby rendering the property unfinanceable, terms are also included that except current or future mortgages from the grantee's liens.

17. Plaque (paragraph 19)

The grantee has the right to install and maintain a small plaque on the protected property. Although the model suggests dimensions, these could be modified depending on the circumstances of the gift, the amount of information that might be included, and the like. For example, rather than place one large plaque on the property, it may be desirable for the grantee to install a series of signs at strategic points on the boundaries of a large estate or rural tract.

The importance of a plaque on the property cannot be minimized. It alerts neighbors and others to the easement and may encourage them to notify the easement grantee in the event they perceive a possible violation. It emphasizes the fact that easements impart certain public benefits and may serve educational purposes. A plaque can also promote the activities of the easement grantee.

18. Runs with the Land (Easement in Perpetuity) (paragraph 20)

The Internal Revenue Code requires that a preservation easement donation be made in perpetuity if a charitable gift deduction is to be claimed by the owner. Paragraph 20 of the model easement document clearly states that the easement agreement "runs with the land" as a binding servitude in perpetuity. However, obligations of any full or partial owner of the property terminate when that person sells or otherwise disposes of the interest in it. Every subsequent owner of the property is bound by the easement terms. Every time the property is sold or leased, a reference to the easement must be provided to the new party in interest.

19. Assignment (paragraph 21)

The easement grantee, as a nonprofit charitable organization under Section 501(c)(3) of the Internal Revenue Code, a qualifying organization under section 170(h) of the Code, and the donee of a qualified charitable preservation easement donation under Section 170(h), is constrained under a number of legal and tax principles in its ability to divest itself of corporate assets, such as preservation easements, to other than charitable organizations. The analysis of these constraints is beyond the scope of this commentary, but they touch on the requirement that easements be donated in perpetuity, potential issues of prohibited private benefit and inurement, implied trust, and others. Therefore, any assignment of the easement can only be to another publicly supported, qualified easement-holding organization. See Treas. Reg. § 1.170A-14(c)(2).

20. Recording and Effective Date (paragraph 22)

The easement document must be recorded to be effective. The recording takes place in the land records of the county (in much of New England, in the town) in which the property is located.

Recording is important to assure that all future owners or potential buyers are given notice of the easement agreement. Once recorded, the existence of the easement will be picked up in any title search. Note that, in at least one instance, the Tax Court held that the easement must be recorded for it to be effective as a *perpetual* restriction as required under Section 170(h)(5)(A) of the Internal Revenue Code. See *Satullo v. Commissioner*, 66 T.C.M. (CCH) 1697 (1993). While *Satullo* involved the interpretation of Georgia law in a case that was complicated by a number of unusual circumstances, it does serve as a warning that an easement may have to be recorded before it is deemed qualified as a perpetual restriction. Therefore, delay in recording the easement until the tax year following its donation may result in the donation deduction being denied until the year of recording. Failure to record entirely may invalidate the donation deduction.

21. Extinguishment and the Stipulated Percentage Value of the Easement (paragraph 23)

Paragraphs 23.1, 23.2, and 23.3 of the model easement document are intended to comply with the easement regulations that specify how proceeds resulting from a subsequent sale or exchange of the protected property after extinguishment of the easement must be shared between the owner and the easement holder. *See* Treas. Reg. § 1.170A-14(g)(6)(ii). There are a number or circumstances in which extinguishment of the easement may occur. For example, if casualty damage to the protected property is so severe that reconstruction of the protected facades is physically or economically impossible, both parties to the easement agreement may want to extinguish it and allow demolition.

The easement regulations allow a preservation easement to be extinguished, but only if the following requirements are met:

- An unexpected change in the conditions surrounding the property make it impossible or impractical to continue to use it for the conservation or preservation purposes;

- The easement is extinguished by judicial proceedings;

- Any proceeds received by the easement holder from a subsequent sale or exchange of the property are used by it in a manner consistent with the conservation of preservation purposes of the original easement donation. See Treas. Reg. § 1.170A-14(g)(6)(i) and (ii).

The regulations also specify the manner in which the easement holder's participation in the proceeds of sale are to be measured. The value of the charitable gift deduction taken by the owner at the date of donation is compared to the market value of the easement-encumbered property as a whole at that date. The ratio becomes the fixed constant that must later be used in allocating the proceeds of an extinguishment between the property owner and the easement holder.

Paragraph 23.2 of the model easement document recognizes the circumstances in which an extinguishment may be possible. The language follows the wording of the regulations and recognizes partial or total destruction of the property as the result of a casualty as one of the "changes in conditions" that may result in extinguishment. The paragraph also makes it clear that the easement holder participates in any net proceeds remaining after payment of costs of the sale and preferential claims or mortgage lenders.

Paragraph 23.3 applies similar rules to the condemnation of property. Paragraph 23.3 recognizes, however, as do the regulations, that state and federal condemnation laws may dictate a different result, thereby disregarding any imputed easement valuation.

The "easement percentage" is made a part of the baseline documentation. In some donation situations, the owner of the property may have a qualified appraisal in hand prior to the date on which negotiations concerning the terms of the easement are completed and the document is recorded. However, federal income tax regulations do not require that the qualified appraisal be obtained by the donor until the date on which a federal income tax return is filed for the year in which the donation was made. Donations are typically made in December, and income tax returns are usually not due until April of the following year (unless the donor receives an extension to file). The donor may not have the completed appraisal report in hand until a few months after the donation date. At that time, the easement percentage would be included in the baseline documentation. If the qualified appraisal were obtained before the date of the donation—tax regulations require it to be completed no earlier than 60 days before donation—paragraph 23.1 could be modified so that the easement percentage is written directly into the easement document rather than included later in the baseline documentation.

22. Interpretation (paragraph 24)

This section of the model easement document is a series of subparagraphs explaining how the wording of the easement document is to be interpreted, and its legal effectiveness. It carefully states that if any portion of the easement document is held to be unenforceable or otherwise illegal, only the suspect portion is affected and not any other portion of the document. It carefully states also that language in the easement document should be interpreted to affect broadly the preservation and conservation purpose of the donation. That is, in effect, an instruction to the courts to try to uphold the easement document from challenge to the extent possible.

Sometimes there may be a conflict between the local building or zoning code and the standards used by an easement holder in enforcing an easement. For example, a particular type of exterior cleaning method or replacement material may be prohibited by a local building code. Paragraph 24(d) encourages the owner of the property to notify the easement holder of any such conflict, and the two parties to the easement agreement are required to cooperate together and with the local government unit to find a compromise solution. Irrespective of this provision, however, if the action of a property owner is either permitted by or not regulated by ordinance or law but nonetheless constitutes a violation of the easement, the grantee may enforce the easement.

The final paragraph also discusses the effectiveness of any future transfer of development rights from the protected property to another parcel. An easement that prohibits demolition often results in a reduction of the development potential of a piece of property. Property value may be seriously affected by the donation. Subparagraph (e) of paragraph 24 recognizes that development potential may be affected by the gift, and states that such development potential cannot be exercised on the property during the term of the easement, nor can it be shifted to an adjacent parcel and exercised if the result of that development would interfere with the preservation and conservation purposes of the easement. For example, a property owner donating an easement that prohibits demolition of a small historic building on a downtown site that is quite valuable for new construction might otherwise be able to acquire an adjacent site, demolish the improvements on that adjacent site, combine it with the easement-protected property into one zoning lot, and develop a new high-rise office building or high-density retail structure to the detriment of the adjacent smaller historic building.

23. Amendment (paragraph 25)

One of the most difficult challenges of easement enforcement and administration is determining when and whether the amendment of an easement is both appropriate and legal. Several organizations have learned—in some cases the hard way—that what may appear to be a simple two-party amendment negotiation may, for both legal and political reasons, involve a number of other participants as well. State easement laws, charitable and public trust law, contract law, and state and federal tax laws that govern the activities of nonprofits may bear on whether and to what extent an easement may be amended. Therefore, even if the easement document contains a provision that authorizes some form of amendment, it will also be necessary to determine what other laws and authorities have to say about easement amendment.

The model easement attempts to address some of the federal tax law issues that govern the administration of easements by publicly supported nonprofit organizations. These are set out in Sections 170(h) and 501(c)(3) of the Internal Revenue Code and include the prohibition on conferring private benefit, the requirement that the easement remain qualified, and the requirement that the conservation and preservation values of the property remain protected. Remember, however, that other considerations will govern the appropriateness of easement amendment as well.

24. Supplementary Mortgage Subordination Provisions (paragraph 26)

In the event the protected property is subject to a mortgage, deed of trust, or other lien, the easement must carefully set out the rights of mortgagees and other lienholders in the property on the date of the donation. The easement regulations require that existing secured lenders (mortgagees) subordinate their rights in the property to the right of the easement recipient to enforce the conservation purpose of the gift in perpetuity. *See* Treas. Reg. § 1.170A-14(g)(2).

However, the alternative paragraph attempts to reconcile the interests of mortgage lenders and those of the easement holder so that the requirement of subordination will not unreasonably interfere with the ability of the property owner to obtain mortgage loans or to obtain the consent of an existing mortgage lender to subordinate. The interest of the mortgage lender is protected in any condemnation proceeding or under any provision of the mortgage loan documents giving the lender the right to receive insurance proceeds as a result of a casualty. The mortgage lender's prior rights to receive leases, rents, or profits from the property as security for a loan are also protected.

The right of a mortgage lender to foreclose on its loan and thereby extinguish the easement is eliminated. The easement survives the mortgage foreclosure, but the responsibilities of the mortgage lender to comply with all easement terms and conditions do not begin until the mortgagee actually becomes the owner of the property following a foreclosure.

About the Authors

Thomas S. Barrett is a lawyer and writer living in Alexandria, Virginia. He was the coauthor, with Janet Diehl, of The Conservation Easement Handbook. *Other legal writings include* The Conservation Easement in California *(with Putnam Livermore) and* Self-Initiation: The Hardrock Miner's Right. *Mr. Barrett was the founding publisher of the quarterly journal* Earth Ethics.

Stefan Nagel is a nationally recognized authority on the private protection of historically, culturally, and environmentally significant properties. He served for nearly fifteen years as legal counsel to The Nature Conservancy and the National Trust for Historic Preservation. He recently associated with one of the nation's leading authorities on private land protection strategies, Stephen J. Small, in Boston Massachusetts. Mr. Nagel authored the sections in The Conservation Easement Handbook *devoted to historic preservation considerations, including the original model historic preservation easement.*